THE WILLOW TEA ROOMS

TEA ROOMS

Recipe Book

Enjoy!

anne x

D1344962

THE WILLOW TEA ROOMS

Recipe Book

CELEBRATING A GLASGOW INSTITUTION WITH
40 RECIPES FOR THE PERFECT AFTERNOON TEA

WITH AN INTRODUCTION
BY ANNE MULHERN

**Wild
Harbour**

First published 2017

Wild Harbour Books
Glasgow
www.wildharbourbooks.co.uk

A CIP catalogue reference for this book is available
from the British Library.

ISBN 978-1-9997189-0-9

Typeset by Andrew Bell Designs in LL Brown,
ITC Cheltenham and Dearjoe 6

Contents

Foreword

I met Anne Mulhern in the mid-1990s. I realised pretty quickly that her intuitive approach to living working heritage was an ideal channel to introduce people to Mackintosh, design and the creative arts more generally.

Taking tea in a Mackintosh tea room allowed Glaswegians, Scots and visitors to taste the 'experience'. This was an early example of how Glasgow has been able to democratise design, the appreciation of the arts and allow everyone to take pleasure in the context, style and a taste of quality leaf tea.

My utilitarian, process led approach to business plans and marketing, (because that's why we met), were always tempered by Anne's passion for the Mackintosh design context. The time she would spend with visitors and locals, patiently guiding then introducing them to the details, sharing favourite areas and communicating her passion for Mackintosh in an unaffected, enthusiastic and joyous manner. However, there is another side to Anne which relates to her obsessive concern with quality and product. For much of her Tea Room career, she has continued to bake, create and coax meringues; in the case of the latter usually from 4 or 5am each morning. For these Tea Rooms are working operations, dealing with volumes seen only in branded chains and the ubiquitous coffee houses. These Tea Rooms have created jobs and nurtured careers, built experience and helped members of staff find a place of employment that was independent, unusual and steeped in Glasgow's proud heritage of design and creativity.

Anne also pioneered tourism marketing cooperation as Treasurer and Chair of Glasgow's Leading Attractions for over a decade. This was the city's first tourism marketing consortia; getting Glasgow visitor attractions to extend the appeal of the city through cooperation. Doing what she has always done, Anne was cajoling and influencing people to work together and build visibility which reaped rewards for all of the businesses involved.

Over the period of the Mulhern–Willow presence, she extended the Tea Rooms at 217 Sauchiehall Street from the initial Room de Luxe onto the Gallery Level, opened tea rooms in Buchanan Street and Watt Brothers retail store and provided museum hospitality at Scotland Street School. All of these laudable achievements, linked by the generation of over 150 full time jobs in the city and areas linked by the design thread of Charles Rennie Mackintosh. Starting back in 1983, Anne successfully operated the Willow Tea Rooms in Sauchiehall Street for some 33 years which merits comparison with Kate Cranston's 24 years at the same location.

Over the years it has been an honour and a pleasure to work with Anne – do enjoy her book and the great recipes included.

Professor J John Lennon
PhD MPhil BSc (Hons)

Director Moffat Centre for Travel and Tourism Business Development
Director of Research
Glasgow Caledonian University

Introduction

It's rare, during a busy working day at the Willow Tea Rooms, that I take time to look back and reflect.

There's always so much to do. Looking after the staff and making sure they have everything they need to do their jobs, checking on production in our in-house bakery, talking to our suppliers about orders or changes to the menu, ensuring our premises are kept in tip-top condition and – most importantly, of course – talking to customers, those I've known for years and those visiting for the first time, catching up and making sure they've enjoyed their visit.

It's been more than 30 years since I opened the Willow Tea Rooms. I was in my twenties, fresh from college, and had no idea what I was letting myself in for. But I had a passion for the brilliance of Glasgow's world-famous architect and designer, Charles Rennie Mackintosh, enjoyed the indulgence of a traditional Afternoon Tea, loved cooking and baking, and had a strong drive to be my own boss.

Since then, we have served well over a million customers. My first premises were within Henderson's The Jewellers flagship store at 217 Sauchiehall Street. This was originally Miss Cranston's Lunch & Tea Rooms, her first full collaboration with Charles Rennie Mackintosh who she had worked with previously. It was the perfect site for me as I was a great fan of both these amazing Glasgwegians. And so my Willow Tea Rooms were born.

My businesses now operate at two other sites. I own the Willow Tea Rooms at 97 Buchanan Street which opened in August 1997 and is next door to the location of one of Kate Cranston's other Tea Rooms. Following the termination of my lease at the building at 217 Sauchiehall Street in June 2016, I was able to keep the Willow Tea Rooms on the same street, relocating to the third floor of another great Glasgow institution, Watt Brothers department store at number 119.

During my 34 years owning the Willow Tea Rooms, my team and I have baked hundreds of thousands of delicious scones, meringues and cakes. We have brewed hundreds of thousands of gallons of refreshing tea. We have cooked and served vast quantities of fine, locally sourced Scottish produce like smoked salmon, bacon, haggis and free-range eggs. And we've provided a home from home for generations of Glaswegians.

As I've travelled in the UK and abroad, sometimes for work and sometimes for pleasure, I've been delighted, when chatting with strangers, to discover that the Willow Tea Rooms is often a familiar name to them. Sometimes it turns out they're regular customers. And it's been a huge pleasure to offer traditional Glasgow hospitality to tens of thousands of international visitors from all across the world, many visiting the city for the first time.

Most important to me, though, have been the long-lasting friendships I've gained through running this business. Whether it's with current staff, some who we've worked with for many years, others who are the sons, daughters, nieces or nephews of former employees, the many fine people who have worked with us in the past and stayed in regular contact, or the huge number of customers who we've got to know well over years, with who we share the ups and downs of everyday life.

So, with more than 30 years behind us, and many more years ahead I'm sure, I thought it was time that we shared my story of the Willow Tea Rooms and some of our favourite recipes. Welcome to the Willow Tea Rooms Recipe Book.

In addition to some of our own most popular cake, savoury and confectionary recipes, we've also asked some of our special friends, a Baker's Dozen of broadcasters, celebrities, superchefs, actors, artists and artisans, to contribute their own recipes for the perfect Afternoon Tea. The result is a unique collection of dishes and treats that are easy to make but will prove mouth-watering for you and anyone you are entertaining for.

But before we get to the recipes, let me tell you the story of how a young woman from the East End of Glasgow, who left school at 15, came to establish a business that is now at the heart of the cultural life of her home city.

Anne Mulhern

Anne, Joanne and Sheila enjoying their tea and scones at their management meeting

Afternoon tea, Mackintosh and me
My story by Anne Mulhern

Let me introduce you to the ten-year-old Anne.

She lives with her Mum, Margaret, and Dad, George, and two younger brothers, George and Marcus, in Carntyne, in the East End of Glasgow.
She goes to St Modan's Primary and, in another year, she'll head to the big school at St Gregory's Secondary. Anne has bags of energy and is always busy. She loves playing with her friends but finds school work really boring.

Her Mum hasn't kept well since her youngest brother was born so Anne helps a lot at home. She enjoys it. She doesn't mind cleaning but loves cooking best. When she gets back from school, it's often her job to get tea ready before Dad gets home from work. It's much more interesting than homework. Anne likes nothing better than when Mum says, 'Oh, you've done that? Aw, thank you so much.'

Dad is an engineer. Once all the family are out at school, her Mum goes back to work in the WD & HO Wills cigarette factory on Alexandra Parade, where she'd worked before marrying George.

When Mum goes back to work she's on shifts, so Anne gets her brothers ready for school in the morning. She always makes sure they've had their breakfast. She likes trying lots of different things in the kitchen, including baking. Even if her cakes don't quite turn out right, Dad is always kind and says how much he enjoys them.

Anne knows she's good at being organised. She even daydreams that one day she might run a bed and breakfast, even though no one in the family has ever had their own business.

• • •

Looking at myself aged ten with hindsight, it's possible to see the foundations being laid for a career in the hospitality business. But back then, to me, it was just normal family life. Like a lot of eldest

Anne (on the right)
with her Uncle Ronnie
and cousin Rona

children, I was expected to help out, and I enjoyed being in charge. I also got bored very easily. I must have driven my Mum and Dad mad at times. I had loads of energy and never stopped. I didn't really take after anyone in the family. So much so, my mother used to say, 'you were drapped doon the wrang lum… where did you come from?'

But I was very well behaved at school, I was never a rebel. Mum and Dad had their rules and you never crossed the line. We were brought up to respect authority and we'd never be cheeky to a neighbour. I was terrified of policemen. It was the way we were brought up. Although I didn't get much out of school, one teacher, Mrs Gillian, a maths teacher, inspired me. She was one of the strictest, but you always knew where you were with her. I would always ask, 'Do you want anything from the shops?' and run errands for her. I always wanted to please.

I left school a few days after my fifteenth birthday. I couldn't wait to leave. We had a neighbour, Charlie, who was a buyer at Goldbergs, the huge department store in Glasgow's Merchant City. I was in the store with my Mum one day and we bumped into Charlie, and I asked him if there were any jobs going. He said he'd ask for me. I started the next day.

I worked in the stock room. If there were returns, I had to get them packaged up to be sent away. I had to help the buyers on the shop floor. Much like school, I was running errands, getting colleagues their lunches from the shops, picking things up and delivering packages.

At Goldbergs, I loved it. I didn't find it intimidating at all, even though I was only 15. The people who worked in my department were very nice, they looked after us juniors. I didn't have too much to do with customers day-to-day but I was nosy, always interested in what they were wearing. I loved getting my little cash envelope at the end of each fortnight, which had the huge sum of £7 in it. That went straight home to my Mum and I got money back for my bus fares and lunch. I did get some spending money, which usually went on clothes. At lunchtime, I'd go to Argyle Street to see what was new in Chelsea Girl and Virgo.

Goldbergs was only a stop gap. When I was 16, I joined WD & HO Wills, the cigarette factory where my Mum worked. At that age I wasn't allowed to work the late or early shift, so I was only on the day shift. I went on an eight-week training course which was required before you could do certain jobs. Wills was a real eye-opener, a very well-run company, and thousands worked there. It was great for the area at that time, Alexandra Parade was really vibrant with lots of shops, kept going by all the workers who had bought flats close by.

I worked on the factory floor for a couple of years then I remember going and sitting an exam. It was a four-hour exam one Saturday morning and there were lots of men who were engineers sitting it too. Somehow, I passed.

Passing the exam meant I could get a job in the office and, with that, I also got overtime, as well as lots of other benefits. It was a fabulous job. It was mostly supporting production with paperwork – everyone had targets. Remember, these were the days before computers so everything that would be done by engineers on their PCs now, had to be done by office staff. The engineers would provide data from particular machines and I had to produce graphs for them, so they could assess performance. I'd also create timesheets and other bits of admin that were handed into payroll. There was a security element to my job as well. In those days, cigarette packets came with special vouchers, a bit like Green Shield stamps, and I had to work on that. They were as good as money so had to be kept under lock and key and everything that was sent out was recorded meticulously.

Although the seventies are famous for strikes and industrial unrest, the relationship with the management at Wills was very good. Everyone was treated with respect.

While I was at Wills, I was still living with my parents. At 18 I took a second job at Maestro's, a nightclub in Scott Street, just off Sauchiehall Street. It had opened in the mid-seventies, on the site of the old Maryland nightclub, where the side entrance to the Centre for Contemporary Art is today. I worked at weekends, from 8.30pm till two or three in the morning. Sometimes when I finished a shift in Wills at 10pm, I'd go to Maestro's and do another shift until three. But when you're young you don't care, you have the energy. I had an aunt who lived in Florida and I wanted to go and visit her, so I was saving up. I also wanted to buy a car. I got a red Morris Marina. My Mum and Dad went halves with me for it. It was second-hand and I loved driving them around in it – neither of them had a licence. And I used to give my younger brothers, George and Marcus, my tips. It was the era of the three-day week and there wasn't much money around, so I wanted to help out.

Maestro's was a high-class place by the standards of the day. It changed my life working there. As a young girl from the East End, I really got to see how the other half lived and it was my first experience of the hospitality industry. I worked behind the bar and then I got given a job behind a desk at the front door, taking the entrance money. There was a lot of pilfering going on so they must have recognised me for the good girl I was. But most of all, I loved talking to all the customers, getting to know them.

An advert for Maestro's nightclub from the Evening Times

The clientele was a real mixture. It was one of the best places to be seen in the late seventies and where all the real posers would go. I'm still friendly with a lot of the people I met during that time. The DJ, Bobby, who I was later married to for seven years, was at Glasgow School of Art studying to be an architect. Through Bobby, and all the people I got to know at GSA, I developed a real love of Charles Rennie Mackintosh. Little did I know then what an influence Mackintosh would have over my future working life.

Maestro's was also a great influence on my family life, as a certain young man, a Mr David Mulhern, also worked there at the same time. We both left Maestro's and went our separate ways, but thankfully we met again many years later. The rest, as they say, is history… we have just celebrated our 25th wedding anniversary and have two amazing grown-up children, Robyn and Ryan, our world. We are so proud of what they have achieved, both have graduated with Honours Degrees from the

The family at Ryan's graduation

University of Strathclyde, something that I could only have dreamed of.

• • •

The big change in my life came in the early eighties when I took redundancy from Wills. It was a tough time in the UK economically and Glasgow was particularly badly affected. A lot of businesses were closing and a lot of people were losing their jobs. Why did I take the risk of leaving a steady job? I don't really know. It was a very intuitive decision, a real gut reaction. It wasn't scientific, I didn't sit and work money out, I just knew it was time to leave.

My main motivation for jumping off the financial cliff was that I wanted to do my own thing. A lot of people were leaving the company at the time. Some people bought a bigger house. But I said, 'I'm putting my money in the bank and I'm going to do something.' Everyone must have thought I'd have that money spent in the first month. It didn't work out that way. I bought a slightly better car,

Anne with Robyn and Ryan

a Vauxhall. I took Mum and Dad out for dinner. I bought an outfit. But the rest stayed in the bank.

I decided to go to college. In those days, you got a grant so I wasn't using up my savings. I went to the Job Centre and the guy asked, 'What kind of job would you like?' And I said that I'd like to go to college. He asked what I wanted to study and I didn't know. He asked what I liked doing, and I said cooking. He said, 'What about the Food Tech?', by which he meant the College of Food Technology. He then asked if I'd like an interview that afternoon. I got interviewed by Peter Cushley, a Senior Lecturer. And, believe it or not, I started on the following Monday. But the most important thing was that I'd found something I really loved.

It was a cookery course involving both theory and practical kitchen work. The lecturers made it clear when we started that, no matter how much cooking we'd done before, everything we knew was wrong and we had to re-learn everything from first principles. It gave us a great foundation.

Anne, her brother George, cousins Rona and Brenda with their Granddad

I also completed an advance bakery course at night and then studied a chocolate and sugar work course. While doing this, I met a lecturer there, Willie McCurrach, who is now Head of Food Studies at the City of Glasgow College, and we've kept in touch over the years. Willie has been a great friend of the Willow Tea Rooms and has always been there for me when I wanted some guidance or advice. Willie knows the business at the sharp end, having worked at the North British Hotel in Edinburgh, making 500 cakes a day from scratch for afternoon tea. I have also kept a close relationship with the current students at the College and every year the best first year full-time student in the Department of Food, within the School of Food, Hospitality and Tourism, wins The Willow Tea Rooms Trophy and Prize.

At the same time as I was studying, I was trying to decide what kind of business I was going to start. I looked at setting up a Patricia Roberts store in the West End of Glasgow. She was a London-based knitting designer who had a chain of high-end knitting shops around the country, selling wool and knitting patterns. But I wasn't that interested in knitting so I worked out that wasn't for me. While I was at college, I realised that what I really wanted was to work in food and hospitality. Whatever I decided to do, it had to be something I was really committed to.

I also spent two days in Milngavie looking at the kind of people who shopped there. Another idea I was thinking about was to set up a health food shop, which were just coming in at the time. I wanted to see who came to the area. Were they young, were they old, how many school kids? I just sat and added them up and made graphs. Why I made graphs I don't know, but it might have come from my time in Wills, seeing how a big company assesses performance.

I used to go down to London for the weekend. I'd drive down to save money and stay in a wee hotel and go shopping. At the time, the Body Shop was the big thing in London, with a flagship store in Covent Garden. I loved it there and bought lots of their products. Naively, I wrote to Anita Roddick and asked about opening a Body Shop in Glasgow. I got a lovely personal letter back from Anita herself, even though the answer was a no. They ended up with 3,000 shops around the world so I was clearly on to something.

With other ideas ruled out, I started to think about opening a tea room. Growing up in Glasgow with my Mum and Gran, we would always go out shopping on a Saturday, and then go for a cup of tea to Frasers, the department store. It was a ritual that I loved. Three o'clock on a Saturday, you would find us upstairs on the third floor having a cup of tea and a cake. Even as a child I knew the places that were busy and those that weren't. Rose, one of the waitresses, was always the draw to Frasers. We'd sit at one of her tables and chat away to her. We also used to go to Treron's, another department store with a tea room, which was beside the McLellan Galleries on Sauchiehall Street. As a young girl, I must have been storing up all that information unconsciously, learning the importance of human relationships and customer service to the business of hospitality.

When it came to a location for my tea room, I wanted something in Glasgow. I loved Glasgow. I loved the city, and although it was the biggest city in Scotland, it was small enough to get about. Big enough and small enough. My family were here.

Anne and her cousin
Rona with their Gran

I didn't have big dreams of going anywhere else, I just wanted to be here.

Glaswegians have a real sense of ownership of their home town. And people who aren't from Glasgow who come to live here end up falling in love with that attitude. I always wanted to stay here. I loved the buildings. I loved other cities. By this time, I'd already been to Barcelona, I'd been to New York. I was 18 when I first went to Florida, I was going to visit my Aunt and Uncle. My first proper holiday wasn't a package holiday. It involved driving with my boyfriend down to London, then on to the ferry, crossing over to France, driving through France and then on to Spain. We ended up in Marbella and then drove all the way back again. I was only 20 at the time, and that was quite cosmopolitan for the late 1970s. I had a real interest in the wider world, I loved going to London. But the other big draw for me back in Glasgow was Charles Rennie Mackintosh. I wanted to bring a traditional tea room to the city using Mackintosh and Kate Cranston as my inspiration. There was nothing like that in the city at the time.

I also wanted a tea room that served proper afternoon tea. I'd been to different hotels, like the Ritz in London and had tried their famous afternoon tea, and I thought it was wonderful. Although I was a Glasgow girl, I was extending my reach, travelling around, seeing what was big in other parts of the country. As a young person visiting London I had developed a little taste for luxury. Maybe I didn't have dinner that night because I'd spent too much money during the day – but you had to get your priorities right. I realised we could provide an elegant, indulgent afternoon tea, here in Glasgow, and my hunch was that Glaswegians would love it.

. . .

At roughly the same time, Hendersons, a top-end

jewellery chain with 20 shops around Scotland, had moved into 217 Sauchiehall Street. They took it on as a flagship store. I knew the building from my interest in Mackintosh. It was the site of one of four Tea Rooms in the city owned by Kate Cranston but was the one in which she had allowed Mackintosh full reign in the design. It still had lots of the original fittings. In the early 1980s Mackintosh's popularity wasn't what it is now but I still thought this would give me a fantastic opportunity to open up his works to, not only locals, but also to a much wider audience of visitors who were keen to explore the city's hidden treasures. It was a gorgeous shop but a lot of Glasgow people were a bit intimidated because it looked so expensive.

It was the glamour of the Mackintosh connection at 217 Sauchiehall Street that made it the perfect site for me. Sauchiehall Street was the main shopping street at the time. Daly & Sons department store had been in the building, they'd been part of the Frasers Group. Daly's was founded in 1934 but had eventually closed in 1979, one of many famous Glasgow department stores that ceased trading in the seventies. I could also see that it would be a big benefit having a huge Marks and Spencers across the road, customers would come across for a cup of tea after they'd finished shopping.

I phoned up the office and asked to speak to Mr Henderson, the owner. I introduced myself and asked if I could meet him. He agreed and when we met I said I'd like to open a tea room in what had been Mackintosh's Room de Luxe, which wasn't being used. He thought it was a very interesting idea, but said no. Why wasn't he interested? He said he was a jeweller and didn't want to get distracted. I took his response on the chin, and went away. But I couldn't drop the idea because I knew it would work for everyone. So, I went back to him, and by this time I'd been speaking to lots of different people and I knew for certain I could make it work. I asked him if he'd let me go and get all the necessary permissions, and then see what happened.

I suppose he didn't think I'd come back. I'm sure he thought I'd lose interest or come up against too many obstacles. He didn't know me from Adam, after all. But he must've seen something in me. He

Hendersons at 217 Sauchiehall Street

said later it was my determination, coming back again after being told no. Eventually, I got a phone call from his wife, Jean, asking to meet for coffee. I had to go to their big house in Ledcameroch Road in Bearsden to meet her. Jean asked me how I'd managed to persuade her husband, Harry, to let me open a tea room in 217 Sauchiehall Street. That was the first I knew that he had agreed.

We started putting in all the plans. Things were slow, but the Council Planning Department bent over backwards to get the building back to having a Tea Room. I had lots of meetings with Environmental Health and people like that. Very naively, I didn't have a shred of self-doubt. This was probably unusual for a woman at that time. I think I've always had a certain amount of natural confidence, although I can look back and remember times when I was also very shy. But my Mum and Dad always encouraged me in whatever I did, so maybe that's where the focus and determination came from.

There weren't any major obstacles, thank goodness. My lecturers at the Food Tech thought I was mad, saying I was going to open up a tea room. But when they saw I was serious, they started to come on board and were a great help. Nothing was a bother, they helped me lay out the tables and helped develop the menu. One of the chefs gave me a carving knife as a present and I still have it to this day. People didn't think I was doing anything special, just opening a wee cafe. But I was so lucky considering the number of people who helped. I wanted to recreate that room as closely to the original Mackintosh designs as possible. Luckily, there were lots of photographs of it. I used to go and meet different academics at Glasgow University and they'd give me prints of the pictures they had so that I could work from them.

We weren't operating on a massive budget. I'd had to go to my bank and apply for a loan and Glasgow Development Agency, the enterprise company, was very supportive. I had to get the replica furniture made and commissioned Keith Gentles, a furniture maker based in Bridge of Allan. There was originally a guy at the Citizens Theatre who was going to make the tables and chairs but that fell through, so we had to ask around to find someone else who could do it. Keith came up trumps. There were a few instances when things didn't go to plan but I just got my head down and found a solution. I managed to find original Victorian cake stands at the Barras. They were only a pound each. They were all a mish mash, no two were the same, but they were totally authentic and gave the right impression.

When I opened up in Sauchiehall Street, I wanted waitress service rather than counter service, which was more common. I wanted to go back to the old-fashioned way. I loved the heritage surrounding tea rooms. I knew the history, that Glasgow invented the concept, going all the way back to when Kate Cranston's brother had a tea merchant's shop in Queen Street. I only found out about Kate later, it was Mackintosh I was interested in first. I had a picture of her in a big crinoline dress – but I didn't learn about her amazing career until later.

Our trademark, the Lady and the Rose, was created by Margaret Macdonald Mackintosh for Kate Cranston's White Cockade Tea Room at the Glasgow International Exhibition

I went to the Hunterian Museum at Glasgow University and met with Pamela Reekie, now retired Professor Pamela Robertson, and she helped me find the image of the Lady and the Rose created by Margaret McDonald, Mackintosh's wife. I decided to trademark it. We needed that on the tables – to make sure the place was keeping with its heritage. I also found an old menu from the original Tea Rooms. It was very small, just a few pages. Mackintosh in the early 1980s wasn't very well known in wider Glasgow, a lot of people from the city didn't know about their world-class designer and architect. When customers came into 217 Sauchiehall Street and came up to the Room de Luxe, they'd look around and gasp. They couldn't believe what they were walking in to. They had no idea such a brilliant gem was so close. We'd get architects from all around the world, and tourists, who knew what to expect, but the local Glaswegians didn't know what they had on their own doorstep.

When we were developing 217 Sauchiehall Street, there were lots of interesting entrepreneurial characters around in Glasgow. David Mullane had opened The Warehouse in Glassford Street. I was a regular customer, it was a favourite place for my Mum and I to visit when we were out shopping together, we loved it there. He was the guy who first brought sparkling bottled water to Glasgow – he was such a forward thinker. I learned a lot from him. And there was Seumas MacInnes at Café Gandolfi, another great favourite of mine. Both The Warehouse and Café Gandolfi had Gaggia coffee machines. There was nowhere on Sauchiehall Street that you could get a cappuccino and so I just had to get a Gaggia machine because I knew how popular this would be. The places that I liked to go to as a customer set the benchmark for me when I opened my Willow Tea Rooms.

■ ■ ■

When we opened on 1st December 1983, it was my 27th birthday. We got our bank manager to come along. We got Jack House, the legendary columnist and author, as well. But at that point I didn't know anyone, we were just being brave – some might call it brass neck... We wrote to Michael Kelly, who was Lord Provost of the city, and asked if he'd like to do the official opening. I realised that, because I had Michael Kelly there, it would get in to the newspapers. I don't know if it was the Lord Provost's office that put out a press release or not, but we got pieces in the *Herald* and *Evening Times*. We hadn't even formally invited the press, we were so naïve. And, because of the newspaper articles, we had a queue of customers waiting when we first opened our doors to the public the following day.

Just like a party, you worry that no one is going to turn up. But it worked brilliantly. I really learned the value of publicity at that point. Ever since, we've welcomed magazine and newspaper photographers who've wanted to use the Tea Rooms as a photoshoot or film location. Others in the city charge an access fee, but we never have. It's free exposure, after all. We'll sing and dance for film crews; we'll sing and dance for anybody who wants to come and take photographs, so long as we're credited. And, of course, we always provide plenty of tea and coffee!

When we opened I decided there shouldn't be any cover charge, no minimum spend, which wasn't common around the city in those days. We were happy for customers to come in at lunchtime, the busiest time, and just have a tea. Some places in Glasgow would insist you had a meal. In my mind, the customer, is always right. It happened sometimes. You'd notice a lady coming in for a cup of tea at lunchtime. But then, a few weeks later, you'd see her in for lunch with a friend and then, after a bit of time, you'd have a very loyal customer. It was a philosophy partly based on my own experience. After all, when you're out you don't always want a big lunch. But it's also a recognition that it's not up to me to tell customers what they can and cannot have.

Right from the very beginning, from the first few weeks, we always asked customers what they thought, the things they liked, the things they didn't like. Not with a questionnaire, but face to face. We asked them if there was anything they'd like to see that wasn't on the menu. We changed quite a lot in the early days based on feedback from customers. Let's face it, one of the great things about Glasgow is that folk aren't shy about telling you what they think.

I used to say to the girls, 'Make sure you keep a notepad, write down what people tell you.' Another idea I picked up from a course I took was that we'd give the staff money to go and have their breakfast somewhere else, at one of our competitors, and when they came back get them to tell us what they liked and disliked. It was very useful for us. Sometimes you could pick up great wee gems. But it was also good for the staff themselves. They could see the things that they personally expected from service and apply it to the way they interacted with our customers. It was a much better way to learn.

I'm also a bit of a magpie when it comes to getting ideas from other businesses. I have a cupboard at home full of things that I've collected when I've been out somewhere else, when I've seen something I liked and thought, that could be good for us. Some things are definitely worth changing for the sake of innovation, but at the Willow Tea Rooms there's always a foundation that is based on traditional values of service and quality.

There was one major casualty during the early years of the business. I got married in 1979, to my first husband Bobby, but we went our separate ways in 1984. The Tea Rooms probably had a lot to do with us splitting up, it was very time consuming establishing a new business. But I loved what I was

The 1996 Mackintosh exhibition at the McLellan Galleries attracted a lot of new customers to the Willow Tea Rooms

Our lights in the Blue Room in Buchanan Street are based on Mackintosh's originals for the Chinese Room in Kate Cranston's Ingram Street tea rooms – note the three stenciled letter Cs for Catherine Cranston Cochrane

doing and couldn't have imagined turning my back on it.

■ ■ ■

Since we first opened in 1983, a great deal has changed. There's a lot more competition in the city, standards have improved across the board, but more visitors are coming to Glasgow too.

As a business, at the start, our only source of income was from the menu. But over the years we have grown our own merchandise significantly. We took it cautiously at the start but it proved very popular. I'm still working with the grandson of a family business, D & C Supplies, who many years ago started supplying mugs to us. And we're still working with a company called Ulster Weavers, over in Northern Ireland. We began by asking if our menu cover would work as a tea towel, and then slowly added other things.

The first time I ordered tea caddies it was a big gamble; we had to take 17,000, and that was only a half order, which they agreed to do if we allowed the order to be manufactured during their quiet period. All the things we had to work out – can we sell all of them? Where do we store them? But we took the risk. It took a couple of years but we sold them all and now caddies of tea are a key part of our range. We've had a few products like that. Another personal favourite is our Glasgow Girl bag, in the style of the famous Bloomingdale's Little Brown Bag. It's very popular with the proud women of Glasgow and we supply it to lots of other outlets across the city.

Glasgow has also changed dramatically since 1983. The skyline has changed, with new museums, housing developments, office buildings, concert venues and bridges. Over the years, there have been some excellent events and festivals that have brought many people into the city and created a new and more vibrant culture; the Garden Festival, the year of City of Culture, the design festivals, and now there's a packed annual programme from Celtic Connections, the Glasgow Film Festival, the Merchant City Festival and World Pipe Band Championships, to all the shows at the Scottish Exhibition and Conference Centre and new Hydro Arena.

The Mackintosh exhibition at the McLellan Galleries in 1996 was a real highlight and great for business. The timing was perfect for us as it coincided with the expansion of the Willow Tea Rooms at 217 Sauchiehall Street onto the mezzanine level of the building. In terms of helping in the renaissance of Glasgow in the late 80s and early 90s, and the rediscovery of Mackintosh by Glaswegians, I was just lucky and in the right place at the right time. We were right across the road from the McLellan Galleries show, almost an extension of it. It was the first time we opened seven days a week. But, for me, it was the Glasgow Garden Festival, back in 1988, that changed everything in terms of Glaswegians' confidence about their own city and identity.

Tastes have developed since we first opened, more than three decades ago. There's much more awareness around dietary requirements so that's something we had to take on board. It's really important to us now and a real plus point in a competitive marketplace. A customer can be sitting with a totally vegetarian afternoon tea and their companion can have a traditional afternoon tea, and it's no big deal at all. We also have a lot more information available relating to allergies and nutrition.

Another big change is that, these days, people quite rightly want to know where we get our ingredients. We get our smoked salmon, which is smoked with Lapsang Souchong tea, from Aberdeen. We make a real effort to source as much as possible locally, both from an environmental point-of-view and also because we can go and check the quality ourselves. We've always been conscious of using local producers but it's something we're much more aware of now. It's also important for international visitors coming to Scotland that they're getting something authentic, that's local to the place they're visiting. They're all relationships that we rely on. Even the eggs we serve on the menu are free-range from a local farm – if we're running out we can just pick up the phone and ask for more – the service they provide is great.

Sometimes customers have questions about the baking and, because we do it ourselves, it's easy to get Amy, our lead baker in Buchanan Street, to come down and have a chat there and then.

Over the years, we have also expanded our tea range hugely. Betty's of Harrogate is famous, so in 1985, I went down to visit them and loved the huge selection of teas that they offered. I spent two days going in and out, seeing how they operated. It was at that point I realised that I needed to go back up to Glasgow and change some of what we were doing. We then converted entirely to loose-leaf tea. The taste is better and there's a real element of theatre involved in brewing, pouring and straining loose tea leaves. These days there's not a tea bag on the premises.

Later, the Tea Council approached me and said, 'We're setting up, would you be interested in getting involved?' It was a trade body comprised of different tea producers, different hotels. We had a tea congress down in Harrogate and every year they'd produce a guide to the best afternoon teas across Britain. It was a great organisation to be involved with and I loved getting a chance to share ideas with other people in the same industry.

The Willow Tea Rooms sign at 97 Buchanan Street

In 1997 I took a gamble and opened a second Willow Tea Rooms at 97 Buchanan Street, next door to the site of another of Kate Cranston's original tea rooms. I had a feeling that things were shifting from Sauchiehall Street. The shops on Buchanan Street seemed nicer, more local, Princes Square had opened, there was more going on. Figures were coming out in the media saying that Buchanan Street was second only to Bond Street in London in terms of retail importance. We also did some market research that told us visitors that came to Sauchiehall Street were also going to Buchanan Street to shop.

The purchase went very smoothly. The only thing was that the building was a shell, even the services had been cut off at the front door and every piece of wiring and copper piping stripped out. There was nothing coming into the building at all. It had previously been computer rooms for the

Bradford and Bingley Building Society next door. There was nothing there; floors and walls were missing so we had to completely gut the building and start from scratch.

The move proved not to be a gamble but a very good business decision. Buchanan Street has grown from strength to strength and every day when I walk into my building, I almost have to pinch myself.

In 2017 we celebrated our 20th anniversary with our customers, in particular everyone had a great day on the 7th August when we had our special Naughty Niceties at Nineties Prices menu – a great success with afternoon teas being the favourite choice.

Over the last three decades, there have also been a number of remarkable opportunities. I got asked to set up a Willow Tea Rooms in Japan. Mackintosh is very well known in Japan. One of the biggest collectors of Mackintosh in the world is a Japanese man and we've always had a lot of Japanese visitors. We were approached by the owners of a chain of restaurants in Japan, the Kozo Fukunaga family, to bring the Willow Tea Rooms there.

Mr Fukunaga's interest in bringing the Willow Tea Rooms to there was related to his own father's relationship with Glasgow. In the 1930s, Mr Fukunaga's father had been awarded the licence to open Lipton Tea Rooms in Japan, which had been the basis for a very successful food and beverage collaboration. The second generation Fukunagas saw the development of the Willow Tea Rooms in Japan as a continuation of his father's legacy, again involving an entrepreneurial Glasgow institution.

It was something that I thought about very carefully for a while. It was a fabulous chance to experience a completely different culture and embrace a real challenge. But, ultimately, I couldn't go ahead. It was the wrong time for me. My children were young and it would have involved spending six months in Japan without them. It's easy to get caught up in the excitement, but a gamble like that has to be right, and if there's any doubt then it's not worth taking the risk.

I did get another chance to go to Japan. One day, in 217 Sauchiehall Street, two men were in and

Anne and her dad celebrating the opening of the Willow Tea Rooms at Watt Brothers – George enjoying his favourite toasted scone with jam.

asked how many tea caddies we could supply for a Trade Fair in Japan. They wanted a lot. We chatted about the Tea Room and then they left and I didn't really think much more about it. Then they got in contact and asked, if they opened a pop-up tea room in Japan during the Fair, would I come and talk at it?

I said yes, of course, expecting to hear nothing more from them. The next day, I got a phone call, confirming the invitation to visit Osaka in Japan, two months later. They arranged flights and a hotel. All they wanted was for me to do a presentation every day and be around the tea room some of the time. My husband, David, of course said, 'You're not going without me!' So, I asked if he could come and they said that if he paid his own flight, of course, there would be no problem. The people we were with were very kind, took us to lots of places. The hospitality was fabulous. This is where I discovered how wonderful green teas are and I realised that that we must introduce them.

Out of the blue in 2004 I received a letter from 10 Downing Street. It told me that I was to be awarded an MBE for Services to Tourism in Glasgow. I was completely taken aback. In fact, I called the telephone number on the letter and told them there must be a mistake. They had got the wrong person! But no, they assured me there was no mistake and this little girl from Glasgow met the Queen in Buckingham Place. I was just so thrilled to be recognised for something I loved doing.

■ ■ ■

I love tea etiquette and the whole culture around tea. There's a great London-based tea writer called Jane Pettigrew and I went along to some of her talks, and we even got her to come to the Tea Rooms to talk about Indian tea. I found her so interesting. I've loved listening and learning about all the subtleties around tea appreciation. I've also learned a lot from our tea suppliers, Thomson's, another company based in Glasgow, that has been importing and blending tea since 1896. Our contact there, Conal, is so consumed by tea, it's wonderful to see. He keeps us right about the best ways to serve different teas in our range. He also introduced us to some great fruit teas, helped us balance our hot teas with a selection of iced teas. He advises a lot on our lines and what we should do with them.

We've undertaken some tea education with the staff and the night we celebrated our 20th anniversary of opening in Buchanan Street, Conal provided some great tea sampling. During the 2014 Commonwealth Games, which were held in Glasgow, Thomson's created a special Commonwealth blend of tea exclusive to the Willow Tea Rooms. We also created a Miss Cranston's tea about three years ago, a specially blended combination of Assam, Darjeeling and Golden Ceylon leaves. Sometimes international visitors take away a particular tea blend and then a few months later we'll receive an email asking us to send more out to them as soon as possible.

A few years ago, we had the chance to operate from another great Mackintosh building, the Scotland Street School Museum, which is now a visitor attraction run by Glasgow Museums. This was a very positive experience for us. It was great

Just some of the teas on offer in the Willow Tea Rooms

to further cement our relationship with Mackintosh. We had the tea room and the shop as well and both were successful. Unfortunately, Glasgow Museums wanted the shop back and sadly, without the shop, the project wasn't commercially viable for us. During our time there, we used the lovely kitchen as our bakery.

Although we've had a very positive relationship with the City Council and its subsidiaries, like the excellent Glasgow City Marketing Bureau, over the years, we have had the occasional disagreement. A key feature of the 1996 Mackintosh Exhibition were the original internal doors from 217 Sauchiehall Street. They toured the world as part of the Mackintosh exhibition but, when they eventually returned home after years away, the Council took them into storage because of the damage that had occurred as part of the normal wear and tear over nearly a century. Although the doors belonged to our landlords at the time, the Council said they had the authority to keep them and put them in a store room. It took years to get them returned. Being part of the then Mackintosh Heritage Group, we had a powerful collective voice, all saying that the doors must be seen in their original location. That was the only thing that made sense. We got them back just before our 25th anniversary of creating the Willow Tea Rooms and were able to celebrate them being back where they belonged for the 2008 Glasgow Doors Open Day Festival. It was so nice to have them back, they should never have left the building. Heritage experts say, as soon as you start stripping one thing out, other things start to disappear. I really believed it was vitally important for the city that the integrity of the interior at 217 Sauchiehall Street was maintained.

■ ■ ■

Although the Willow Tea Rooms has been running for well over 30 years, I never stop looking at what we are doing and how we are doing it. The hospitality business is constantly changing and we have to make sure we keep up. To help me do this, in 2008 I brought in a Business Manager, Sheila Proctor, whose job is to make sure that all the back-office functions support me and the team to deliver exceptional customer service.

To run a successful kitchen and a bakery you have to keep watching and listening. It's crucial to make sure standards are maintained and, as the owner, that's one of my most important jobs. It's also essential to listen to customers. They'll tell you if things aren't right but you have to be listening. It's easy for the customer's voice to be drowned out amongst all the other things competing for your attention.

I continue to be a great believer in watching what's happening in the wider world. I keep reading newspapers and magazines, buying the latest cookery books, in order to keep up with current trends, what cakes people are talking about and what's currently popular. Although traditional values are at the heart of what we do, we'll never be old-fashioned.

To run a bakery, you've got to have staff who love baking. I used to do all the baking myself and, although I loved it, as the business grew, it was too big a job for one person. Now we have a great team of bakers, with a real passion. The Great British Bake Off has had a huge impact and we find that customers are more knowledgeable now. They recognise what's in the cake cabinet more readily and know what they want. So, we need to make sure they get it.

At the heart of my philosophy and something I always say to staff is, 'Don't serve anything you wouldn't be happy to eat or drink yourself.' It sounds obvious, but that approach has to be maintained. We are the 'world-famous' Willow Tea Rooms after all, we have a reputation to maintain, something to live up to, which is great motivation for everyone. But we'll never remain successful unless we build strong relationships with our staff members. We rely on them so much it'd be impossible not to.

Ultimately, I want customers who visit the Willow Tea Rooms to say that they had a really great time, they enjoyed the experience here – that's what makes me smile. Just like my Mum saying, 'thank you' all those years ago. We achieve that through service, the quality of the food on offer and the atmosphere we create. These are the most important things for customers.

It seems like a lifetime ago that I set out on this journey, and it seems like yesterday too. When I was a young girl I had no idea where life would take me, but I'm sure ten-year-old Anne would approve. I wouldn't say I'm the most academic person but I've been blessed with common sense, which is the foundation of any business. And I've always followed my instincts. I've been incredibly lucky to run a thriving enterprise that's become a focal point for the people of Glasgow and for those visiting us. I've been lucky to be able to share my passion for a world-class architect and designer, Charles Rennie Mackintosh, and for the city that created him. If I have helped others appreciate his talent then that makes me happy too.

Why are Glasgow people like me so proud of their city? It's born in us and it's in our blood, it must happen in the maternity hospitals. We stick together. And, make no mistake, our hospitality is second to none.

Anne with Marie and
Jeanette enjoying their
afternoon tea

An extraordinary partnership

Miss Cranston and Charles Rennie Mackintosh

Catherine Cranston, or Kate as she was known, founder of four very different and unique Tea Rooms in Glasgow, was a hugely successful entrepreneur during the late 19th and early 20th centuries.

She broke the mould as a dynamic, creative and driven businesswoman in an age when women were not only discouraged from commerce but met with outright hostility and social disapproval. Known for her eccentric and slightly old-fashioned but flamboyant dress sense and ebullient personality, she established the Tea Rooms as an integral part of daily life in her home city, creating the very best and most innovative examples, leading the market for decades, her name a byword for sophistication, elegance and value. But she was, perhaps most importantly, the one single individual most responsible for nurturing the extraordinary genius of Glasgow's greatest designer and architect, Charles Rennie Mackintosh, a talent of global significance.

Kate Cranston was born into a family of hoteliers in 1849. Her father, George, had a succession of hotels around George Square. Her Uncle, Robert, founded the Waverley Temperance Hotels in Edinburgh, where the Old Waverley at 42–44 Princes Street, opened in 1845, still operates today. Kate's brother, Stuart, had a tea retailing business at 2 Queen Street, Glasgow, founded in 1871, and can rightly claim to have invented the Tea Room when he first started charging for tastings of his product in 1875, selling bread and cakes on the side. The innovation proved hugely popular and his sister saw its commercial possibilities.

In her late twenties, Kate Cranston started her own Tea Room with investment from her Uncle Robert. He'd already helped set up Kate's cousin, Mary, in business, running her own hotel in Edinburgh. Kate's Crown Tea Rooms opened for business in 1878 on the ground floor of a temperance hotel in Argyle Street. Despite this being the year of the collapse of the City of Glasgow Bank, ruining many, the business thrived and within eight years she was ready to open a second, this time at 205 Ingram Street. At a time when fashion demanded that dinner was taken later and later into the evening, the Crown Luncheon Rooms targeted hungry businessmen and clerks needing fed during the working day. The absence of alcohol and carefully considered interior design ensured it was regarded as 'respectable' by the burgeoning middle classes, cementing its popularity.

The last quarter of the 19th century was a time of significant social change, not just in Glasgow but across the UK. One innovation in Kate Cranston's Tea Rooms, as well as others, was rooms for women as well as for men. As social conventions eased a little, and at a time when the department store was coming into its own, women needed suitable places to go for refreshment and 'comfort' while out shopping. Of course, pubs and inns were no places for ladies. Recognising this growing market, Cranston placed increasing emphasis on the interior design of her establishments, realising this was an important point of difference in a competitive marketplace.

In 1888, the year of Glasgow's first great international exhibition, Cranston undertook refurbishments of both her businesses. In Argyle Street she took more risks, employing the 21 year-old George Walton, younger brother of the 'Glasgow Boy', artist EA Walton. George Walton was a talented amateur interior designer, taking evening classes at the Glasgow School of Art while working in a bank, and was influenced by William Morris, John Ruskin and the Arts and Crafts Movement. Walton would contribute greatly to the establishment of what became known as the 'Glasgow Style'. His commission by Cranston helped him launch a highly successful professional career in applied arts and architecture.

Glasgow continued to develop commercially, with the population of the city growing dramatically every decade towards the end of the century and beyond. In 1892, Kate married a prosperous industrialist, John Cochrane, eight years her junior,

The artist, Margaret Macdonald, Mackintosh's wife and long-time creative collaborator

Charles Rennie Mackintosh

who owned an engineering works in Barrhead. Rather than giving up work, as convention demanded, Cranston's business empire could now expand with the support of her husband's wealth. Equally unusual, she retained her maiden name in business, as Miss Cranston's Tea Rooms by now were known city-wide.

In 1896, Kate Cranston acquired four floors of a brand-new building on Buchanan Street. She employed George Walton to undertake the huge interior decoration project. To help him, she commissioned a 28 year-old graduate from the Glasgow School of Art to design murals on the walls surrounding a lightwell over three floors. His name was Charles Rennie Mackintosh and he worked for the architectural practice, Honeyman and Keppie. The murals were in a new and radical avant-garde style that Mackintosh and his group – which included his future wife, Margaret Macdonald – championed. On completion, the work immediately attracted praise from art critics as something fresh and exciting.

Once Buchanan Street was fully established, Kate returned to her first business in Argyle Street. Rather than reworking the tea rooms on the ground floor, she took over the entire building. It's said that the lease had been a wedding present from her husband. After the façade had a facelift, Walton was employed to refurbish the decoration and fittings while Mackintosh was commissioned to design the furniture. He created 16 separate designs, including stools, tables, hat stands and his first, iconic and now instantly recognisable high-backed 'Mackintosh' chair.

The new Argyle Tea Rooms opened in 1899 and in 1900 Kate Cranston commissioned both Mackintosh and his new wife to create a ladies' luncheon room and a basement billiard room in her Ingram Street establishment, which

Chinese Room, Ingram Street, Cash Desk

White Dining Room,
Ingram Street

was expanding after she'd acquired a next-door
shop. George Walton had moved to London in 1897
so the Mackintoshes had complete creative control.
In the luncheon room Charles and Margaret created
a decorative panel each as companion pieces that
faced each other across the room, his being The
Wassail, hers was called The May Queen. Both are
high art nouveau and unmistakably 'Mackintosh'
in style. The couple designed every other element
of the interior from panels, screens and glass
to furniture and lighting. Charles had originally
estimated the work would take three to four
months but it took the best part of a year. A year
later, Charles Rennie Mackintosh was promoted to
partner, his firm renamed as Honeyman, Keppie
and Mackintosh.

The high-water mark of Kate Cranston's
collaboration with Mackintosh began in 1902 with
the purchase of a new site at 217 Sauchiehall Street,
which would become Miss Cranston's Lunch and
Tea Rooms. Sauchiehall means 'a damp place where
willows grow', and this inspired Mackintosh to
incorporate the Willow theme throughout his work
in this building. He was given control of not only
the interior decoration but the architecture as well.
He created the distinctive white render façade with
asymmetric leaded windows, including a huge bay

Miss Cranston's
Buchanan Street
Tea Rooms with
Mackintosh's wall
murals

window on the first floor, contrasting with the more
restrained sandstone buildings all around.

The interiors of the Tea Rooms were the height
of sophistication, with white, pink and silver used
for the ladies' areas and grey canvas panelling and
pink stencilling in the rear dining area. Mackintosh
created two main chair designs, a high ladder-
backed dining chair and contrasting low, square
armchair, both dark stained. But the highlight
was the Salon de Luxe, an enclosed space on

the first floor where prices were higher. It was a masterstroke of marketing by Kate Cranston and its exclusivity proved irresistible for fashion-conscious Edwardians. It became known as the 'Room de Looks', as much for its hand-picked waitresses as for the glamorous clientele. The interior was the height of luxury, with dramatic stained-glass doors, a mirrored stained-glass frieze and high-backed chairs painted silver and inlaid with purple glass. While working alongside Mackintosh, Margaret also contributed a frieze called O Ye, All that Walk in Willowwood that faced the Salon de Luxe's fireplace.

The Tea Rooms opened to acclaim in October 1903. The Evening News described it as, 'the acme of originality', while the Bailie stated, 'it fairly outshines all others in matters of arrangement and colour'. In 1904 Kate Cranston asked Mackintosh to design the interior and furnishings of her new marital home, Hous'Hill at Nitshill on Glasgow's southern edge.

After the Tea Rooms, and having completed other major works, including his 'masterpiece', the Glasgow School of Art, the Scotland Street School and Hill House at Helensburgh, Mackintosh found new commissions increasingly difficult to come by. But Kate Cranston continued to find projects for them to work on together. She commissioned him to create a new tea room in the basement of the Argyle Street premises in 1905 and, in 1907, a billiard room and Oak Room in an extension at Ingram Street, followed by the Oval Room and a ladies' rest room two years later. In 1911, she commissioned both Charles and Margaret to help create the temporary White Cockade Tea Rooms at the Scottish National Exhibition. In 1911, she also commissioned Mackintosh to create two new rooms in Ingram Street, the Chinese Room and the Cloister Room. Both use strong colour and mirrored glass while experimenting with an interesting new material, plastic.

In 1913 Mackintosh was forced to resign from Honeyman and Keppie. Since the middle of the previous decade he'd become depressed and had been drinking heavily, while failing to attract work at the levels of previous years. In 1914, just before the outbreak of the Great War he and his wife left

Glasgow for an extended holiday. They would never return to Scotland. In 1916 Kate commissioned one final project, an underground extension to her Tea Rooms in Sauchiehall Street, named the Dug-Out. Mackintosh's designs included geometric furniture painted yellow-gold.

A few months after the Dug-Out opened, in the summer of 1917, John Cochrane died. Kate was heartbroken, selling all her businesses, the family home and its contents. She ended her days living in the North British Station Hotel on George Square, a few hundred yards from where she'd been born. Mackintosh died of cancer in France in 1928. Cranston outlived him by six years, leaving a fortune when she eventually died in 1934, a few weeks short of her 85th birthday.

Kate Cranston transformed Glasgow at a time of great economic and social upheaval and, through her financial acumen, strength of personality, natural entrepreneurship, nose for talent and commitment to art and design, achieved great success in an age when women were all but excluded from business. She also made a huge contribution to the development of one of Scotland's greatest artists. Kate Cranston's life is one of Glasgow's most inspiring stories and she continues to be an inspiration for everyone at the Willow Tea Rooms today.

A brief history of tea

"If you are cold, tea will warm you;
if you are too heated, it will cool you;
if you are depressed, it will cheer you;
if you are exhausted, it will calm you."

– William Gladstone

In comparison with its European and North
American neighbours, Britain is a nation of tea
drinkers. But tea was adopted relatively late in our
history. The first printed reference to tea comes
from 1598 where it was described as *chaa*, coming
from the Cantonese for tea, *cha'a*, which became
char in English. The word tea originates from the
dialect of Amoy, now Xiamen, in the south east of
China, and *t'e*. Tea cultivation in China and Japan
goes back thousands of years and was encouraged
by monks as a means of curbing the consumption of
alcohol, much as it was by the British temperance
movement in the 19th century.

While the Portuguese were the first Europeans
to discover Chinese tea, it was the Dutch who first
imported it, a shipment arriving in 1610. The first
advert for tea appeared in a British newspaper in
1658 and the famous diarist, Samuel Pepys, tried his
first cup in 1660. By this time coffee had established
itself as the drink of choice in the British Isles,
with men-only coffee houses, known as 'penny
universities', being opened for business in major
cities. Initially, it was these coffee houses that
promoted tea as an alternative to their staple, but
tea wouldn't establish itself in the national psyche
until the mid-18th century.

The vast majority of tea was imported from
China by the East India Company. In 1664,
they placed an order for 100 lbs, to meet court
demand stimulated by Charles II's Portuguese
wife, Catherine, who had a taste for tea. In 1717,
the enterprising Thomas Twining started selling
imported tea direct to householders by weight
and its popularity grew. By 1750 East India was
importing almost 5,000,000 lbs a year.

THE TEA PHRENSY.

An 18th century cartoon making fun of the popularity of tea

In the 18th century, as the craze for tea took hold, Parliament imposed huge taxes on tea leaves. Despite being ruinously expensive, it remained popular in all sections of society. The French aristocrat La Rouchefoucauld, after a visit across the Channel, said, 'Throughout the whole of England the drinking of tea is general. You have it twice a day and though the expense is considerable, the humblest peasant has his tea just like the rich man.'

Tea was guarded jealously and every home had a lockable tea caddy. Those rich enough to have staff would get first use of tea leaves before passing them on to their servants. Once the servants had brewed them a second time, they would be sold at the back door for further use.

Smuggling in tea became highly profitable. Black market tea was often cut with *smouch*, an appetising mixture of Ash leaves steeped in green iron sulphate crystals and sheep dung. Having been granted a monopoly over the importing of tea to the Americas by Parliament in 1773, mainly to offset the loss of profits to smuggling, the East India Company's exorbitant import duty met with outrage, prompting the Boston Tea Party and igniting the American War of Independence. This is the most likely reason why the United States is now a nation of coffee drinkers.

In 1833, partly because of a trade war with China and an end to its monopoly, the East India Company's interest in Chinese tea started to wane. A decade before, the Scotsman, Robert Bruce, had discovered a native Indian tea bush in Assam. After his premature death, his brother Charles Alexander Bruce, took over the project and in 1839 Indian tea was launched on the British market. By the final quarter of the 19th century, demand for Chinese tea had plummeted and Indian tea ruled supreme.

There are more than 3,000 different teas produced in many places around the world, all made from one plant, the *Camellia sinensis*. The plant has two subspecies, one of which is able to withstand cold climates and the other that flourishes in hot, tropical locations – it is amazing to think that one plant can produce so many different varieties, indeed it has been likened to the grape which produces so many different types of wine.

There are six very distinct types of tea – black, green, flavoured, oolong, white and compressed. All coming from the one bush, it's the manufacturing process that produces the different types.

Tea is very much a natural product which contains no preservatives, no artificial colourings or additives (other than of course the flavourings which are added to flavoured teas) and, without adding milk or sugar, is virtually calorie free. Tisanes make a very refreshing alternative to traditional teas and have no caffeine content, something which is becoming more and more popular today.

Glasgow has a great affinity with tea, both as tea drinkers and innovators, and the city took a lead in the history of the industry. Glasgow was the birthplace of one of the most successful tea exporters and importers, Sir Thomas Lipton, born in 1848 in the Gorbals, whose company still sells over ten million cups of tea a day in North America.

Because tea is a seasonal crop, getting imported tea to market fast gave 19th century importers huge commercial advantage. They commissioned the construction of Tea Clippers, ultra-fast sailing ships designed to land tea back in Britain first. Many of the finest Clippers were built in shipyards located on the River Clyde, Glasgow's famous river.

During the Great Tea Race of 1866, many of the Clyde-built Clippers won prizes, a fantastic testament to the skill of all those who worked in the shipyards at this time.

How to make the perfect cup of tea
– Always use loose leaf tea if you can, the best quality you can afford
– Keep the tea in an airtight container or tin tea caddy
– Always use fresh water and the softer the water the better the tea will taste
– Never re-boil water
– Warm the pot first
– Once the kettle has boiled let it sit for a minute before pouring into the teapot – otherwise the water may scald the leaves, impairing taste
– One spoonful of loose tea per person plus one extra for the pot
– Leave the tea to infuse in the pot for five minutes before straining
– Add milk before or after you pour – it doesn't matter
– Top up the teapot with boiling water when it is half empty

Should we add milk, lemon or leave tea black? The Chinese were the first to be observed adding milk to tea by a Dutch ambassador to Canton in 1655. And lemon was introduced by Queen Victoria, but was originally a Russian habit, who were also known to stir jam into their tea. The general rule of thumb is that milk or cream with black tea is down to personal taste. But tea tasters recommend taking green or oolong teas without.

On the question of how to prevent the second half of any pot tasting stewed, Mrs Beaton, author of *The Book of Household Management*, recommends using two pots. Once the first cups have been poured she suggests straining the remaining tea into a second warmed pot, thus preventing further infusion.

On a summer's day, afternoon tea in the garden was the height of sophistication

Afternoon Tea

In the early 1800s, tea drinking habits started to change when Anna, the 7th Duchess of Bedford, took to drinking tea with a light snack in the middle of the afternoon, to fill the gap between early luncheon and late dinner. She found a pot of tea served with some bread and butter around four o'clock was the ideal pick-me-up. She loved the idea so much and found it so satisfying that she started inviting friends to join her for tea in the middle of the afternoon.

As the 1800s continued, tea drinking became an essential part of the social scene for all ages. Tea parties were arranged for every possible occasion. By the end of the 19th century fashion designers were creating beautiful gowns for the ladies to wear at teatime, and housekeeping manuals and cookery books were giving lots of details on teatime invitations, etiquette, methods of brewing and serving tea, tablewares, dress, menus and food presentation.

During the 20th century, tea rooms opened up all over Britain where people could go and enjoy tea with hot and cold, sweet and savoury foods. Some of the large hotels also had entertainment, which the ladies and gentlemen could enjoy while sipping their tea from fine bone china cups and nibbling dainty cucumber and smoked salmon sandwiches.

Today, afternoon tea is one of the most popular social events across all ages. It consists of three key elements, neat finger sandwiches, scones with jam and clotted cream, pastries and cakes, all served with a pot of refreshing tea (or of course coffee!).

Savouries

...

Asparagus Canapes
by Greg Taylor

Serve warm or cold. Delicious with a gin and tonic!

Ingredients

12 new season asparagus spears

6 slices Parma ham, cut each slice in half

olive oil

salt and ground black pepper

Prep: 10 minutes

Cook: 10–15 minutes

Method

Preheat oven 180C/160CFan/Gas4.

1. Trim ends of asparagus (I prefer the fat ones that way you only need one spear per serving, if it is skinny ones use two).

2. Wash and trim the bottom ends.

3. Boil the asparagus for 3–4 minutes, pat dry, then wrap one slice of Parma ham round each spear tightly.

4. Place on baking tray, brush with olive oil, season with salt and black pepper.

5. Bake in the oven for 15 minutes for thick stalks and 10 minutes for thin stalks.

Greg Taylor

Greg and I have been friends for 30 years and have enjoyed many a trip together. He's a fantastic host, it's always a pleasure to spend a night at his house. He's also a great hairdresser – Greg is a partner in Creswell & Co, the salon in Glasgow's West End.

Easy Peasy Blinis
by Archie Forrest

Makes approx 16

Ingredients

1 cucumber

packet of cocktail blinis – usually 16 (if you want to make your own see below)

1 lemon

1 packet of Scottish smoked salmon

sour cream

salt and ground black pepper

dill or chives

Prep: 30 minutes

Cook: 5 minutes

Blinis

12.5g yeast

350g plain flour, sifted

285ml milk, lukewarm

2 free-range egg yolks

a pinch of salt

145ml milk, tepid

2 free-range egg whites, whisked

Prep: 30 min to 1 hour

Cook: less than 10 min

Method

1. Cut ends from cucumber to form cylinder.

2. Cut ribbons from cucumber with the peeler until you hit the seed core. The cylinder will become square.

3. Put ribbons into a bowl and add a tablespoon of sour cream. Squeeze the juice from ¼ lemon into the bowl. Too much will make it too watery. If you like a stronger lemon zing add some zest. Season with salt and ground pepper.

4. Cut smoked salmon into 4cm squares.

5. I like to heat blinis before assembling. Place blinis on a separate plate for this. Coil single ribbon of cucumber to form mound on warm blini. Place one or two squares of salmon on top, followed by a few turns of course ground black pepper. If you want to impress, add a sprig of dill or some cut chives.

For the blinis (makes approx 32)

If you have too many put the spares into the freezer. When you take them out of freezer, pop in oven for a few minutes.

1. Make a thin paste out of the yeast and 225g of the sifted flour diluted with the lukewarm milk.

2. Leave this paste to ferment for two hours in a warm room, and then add the rest of the flour, the egg yolks, a pinch of salt, the tepid milk and mix together. Finally add the whisked egg whites.

3. Let the preparation ferment for half an hour, cook the blinis quickly in a small pan.

Archie Forrest

Archie is Scotland's leading contemporary Colourist painter, a former tutor at Glasgow School of Art, but more importantly to me a great friend and neighbour. I have enjoyed many wonderful times at Archie's home.

Cheese and Chive Scones by Kirsty Wark

To make 8 Scones – delicious with a glass of chilled Chardonnay or a rich Merlot

Ingredients

225g plain flour

Pinch of sea salt

1 level teaspoon bicarbonate of soda

1.5 level teaspoon cream of tartar

Half a teaspoon of dried English mustard

180g Barwheys cheddar, 90g finely grated, 90g roughly chopped

2 tablespoons fresh chopped chives

25g unsalted organic butter

150ml milk (you might not need it all)

1 medium free-range egg, beaten with a little milk

2 russet apples

Prep: 15 minutes

Cook: 10 minutes

Method

Preheat oven 220C/200CFan/Gas7.

1. Sift the flour, salt, bicarbonate of soda, cream of tartar and dried mustard into a bowl.

2. Rub in the butter until the mixture resembles fine breadcrumbs.

3. Add 90g of very finely grated cheese, 90g of chopped cheese and chives.

4. Gradually add sufficient milk to make a soft but not sticky dough.

5. Turn the dough onto a floured surface and knead lightly then roll the dough out into a thickness of just less than an inch.

6. Use a 6cm cutter to cut the scones.

7. Put on a floured baking tray and glaze with the eggy milk.

8. Bake for 10 mins.

To serve, finely slice the russet apples and fan half a dozen slices on the plate with the cheese scone and a small pat of French salted organic butter.

Kirsty Wark

A Scottish journalist, Kirsty is best known for hosting BBC Two's news and current affairs programme, *Newsnight*. A neighbour and friend, Kirsty is a past Celebrity Masterchef contestant where she reached the final. In her spare time, you will always find Kirsty in her kitchen – a woman after my own heart.

Choux Buns Filled with Chicken Liver Pate by AJ Morris

15 Mini Choux Buns

Ingredients

75ml water

75ml milk

60g unsalted butter

Pinch salt

75g sieved plain flour

2 medium free-range eggs lightly beaten

Prep: 30 minutes

Cook: 25 minutes

Method

Preheat oven to 200C/180CFan/Gas 6.

Grease baking sheet, run under cold water then tap to get rid of excess water.

1. Bring the water, milk, butter and salt slowly to the boil in a medium pot, keep stirring so the butter melts before it boils.

2. Take pan off the heat and add all the flour, stir to form a smooth paste. Return to a low heat, stir constantly until a ball is formed.

3. Transfer to a bowl and cool for about 5 minutes, then gradually add the eggs, ensuring they are absorbed into the paste. It should have a dropping consistency.

4. Fill a piping bag fitted with a 2cm nozzle with the paste and pipe little balls about the same size as a cherry tomato.

6. Bake until risen for 10 minutes, then increase temperature to 220C/200CFan/Gas7 for a further 15 minutes.

7. Pierce the side of each one to let out steam, cool on a wire rack.

8. Once cooled, fill with the pate.

AJ Morris

I met AJ when she was a student at the Food Tech and did a placement with me at the Willow Tea Rooms in Sauchiehall Street during my first year of operation. A brilliant worker, so keen and enthusiastic, we have remained in touch since that time and am so pleased to see AJ as part of a very successful business at St Bride's Poultry.

Chicken Liver Pate

Ingredients

200g chicken livers, cleaned with membrane removed

175ml milk

75g butter melted

I teaspoon olive oil

1 shallot peeled & finely chopped

1 clove garlic, crushed

3 sprigs of thyme, picked

125ml brandy or port

Pinch of mace

100ml double cream

Salt and ground black pepper

Prep: less than 30 minutes plus couple of hours soaking

Cook: less than 30 minutes

Method

1. Place chicken livers in a bowl, pour over milk and place in the fridge for a couple of hours, this helps to take away any bitterness from the livers.

2. Drain, rinse and pat dry the livers.

3. Heat the oil in a sauté pan and gently fry the shallot and garlic until soft. Remove from pan and set aside.

4. While the onions are softening put the brandy or port into a small saucepan and reduce by half.

5. Once onions and garlic are cooked, remove from the pan, give it a quick wipe then turn up the heat, add the livers and thyme. Do not overcook the livers as they will become grainy, pour in the reduced alcohol.

6. When just cooked put into a food processor along with the onions and mace and blitz to a puree.

7. While processor is running, add in the melted butter.

8. Check seasoning and add salt and pepper to taste.

9. Sieve into a bowl and, when cool, cover and chill until ready to use.

10. Before filling the choux buns, whip the cream until soft, you don't want it to be stiff.

11. Gently mix as much softly whipped cream into the pate as is needed for a good consistency to pipe easily into the buns, while still holding its shape.

Crab Cakes

Makes 12 – Makes a terrific sandwich if you're on the move!

Ingredients

454g bag crab meat
(I get this from my
fishmonger)

200g mashed potatoes

2 spring onions, finely
chopped

2 tablespoons flat
leaf parsley or chives,
chopped

5ml English mustard

5ml Lea and Perrins
Worcester sauce

5ml mayonnaise

Dash Tabasco

Salt and ground black
pepper

1 large free-range egg
and milk for egg wash

Breadcrumbs

Prep: 20–30 minutes

Cook: 20 minutes

Method

1. Combine the crab meat, potatoes, spring onion, parsley or chives, mustard, Lea and Perrins, mayonnaise and Tabasco.

2. Season with salt and ground black pepper.

3. Shape into 5cm cakes.

4. Egg wash and dip into breadcrumbs.

5. Shallow fry in oil over a medium heat for about 5 minutes each side.

Serve

With a lemon mayonnaise.

Cullen Skink

Serves 4-6 – Great with Lorraine's soda bread recipe

Ingredients

50g butter

50g flour

2 leeks, finely chopped

425ml creamy milk

2–3 tablespoons of double cream

500g floury potatoes such as Maris Piper or King Edwards, peeled and diced

300ml chicken stock

500g undyed smoked haddock fillet

8 tablespoons chopped parsley plus a little extra to garnish

Salt and freshly ground black pepper

Prep: 10 minutes

Cook: 30 minutes to 1 hour

Method

1. Melt the butter in a pan, add the leeks and cook gently for 7–8 minutes until soft but not browned.

2. Add the flour and stir to make a roux.

3. Pour in the milk slowly, stir or whisk, and bring to the boil.

4. Add the stock and diced potatoes, stir and simmer for 20 minutes until they are really soft.

5. Skin and chop the smoked haddock and place in the pot, bring to the boil, simmer until the fish is cooked.

6. Stir in the cream and the parsley and season to taste.

Serve garnished with a little more chopped parsley.

Cheese and Broccoli Quiche
Dough enough for 12 mini quiche

Ingredients

Pastry

180g plain flour

100g cold butter, cut into cubes

50g parmesan cheese, grated

1 medium free-range egg yolk

1 teaspoon ice cold water

Filling

3 medium free-range eggs

3 tablespoons double cream

½ head of broccoli

85g gruyere cheese, plus 20g to sprinkle over

Prep: 15 minutes plus resting time

Cook: 40 minutes

Notes

For gluten free option, substitute the plain flour for gluten free plain flour

Method

Preheat oven to 180C/160CFan/Gas4.
Grease a 12 cup muffin tin.

1. Rub butter into flour until the mixture resembles breadcrumbs.

2. Add the parmesan, then egg yolk and water until the dough forms a ball.

3. Wrap the pastry in cling film and chill in the fridge for half an hour.

4. Roll out your pastry, using a pastry cutter, cut discs of pastry to fit your muffin tin. The sides must be high to hold the filling.

Make the filling

1. Blanch the broccoli florets for 2–3 minutes until tender, drain.

2. Beat the eggs and cream, add a pinch of salt and pepper, then add the broccoli and cheese.

3. Take the muffin tin lined with pastry, cover with cling film and fill with baking beans.

4. Place the tin on a tray and pop into the oven for 10–12 minutes, remove the beans and cook for another 10 minutes until golden.

5. Pour the filling into the baked pastry case and bake for 20 minutes until golden brown.

Mushroom and creamy spinach mini filo tartlets

Makes 12 minis

Ingredients

1 packet of Jus-Rol filo pastry, 270g

Olive oil for brushing

25g Stork margarine (block)

1 red onion, finely chopped

⅓ teaspoon smoked paprika

⅓ teaspoon cayenne pepper

150g chestnut mushrooms, medium, quartered

½ teaspoon grated nutmeg

200g soya cream

200g baby leaf spinach

Prep: 30 minutes

Cook: 20 minutes

Method

Preheat oven to 190C/170CFan/Gas5
Prepare 12 hole muffin tin.

1. Cut the filo into 12x12cm squares, brush the tin with the oil all over the inside of the holes, then line each hole with a square of filo.

2. Brush the inside of the pastry sparingly with oil and repeat until you have three layers in each hole, finish with a light brush of oil. Put the layers at different angles to each other in the holes.

3. Bake the filo cases at 190C/170CFan/Gas 5 for 7–9 minutes until golden brown.

4. Place the stork into a saucepan and melt over a low heat. Add the onion and cook gently for 2–3 minutes without colouring. Stir in the smoked paprika and cayenne pepper.

5. Add the mushrooms and put the lid on the pan. Cook gently for a further 3–5 minutes.

6. Stir in the nutmeg, soya cream and spinach. Cook covered, over a gentle heat, for 10 minutes, then remove the lid and cook for a further 10 minutes until the spinach is wilted and tender and the soya cream has reduced slightly.

7. Spoon the mixture into the prepared tartlet cases and serve.

Lentil Pate with Oatcakes

Serves 4-6

Ingredients

Lentil Pate

1 tbs olive oil

2 cloves garlic, minced

1 red onion, finely chopped

1 carrot, finely chopped

1 stalk of celery, finely chopped

1 tbs tomato puree

1 tsp ground coriander

½ tsp cayenne pepper and ½ tsp cumin

Sprig of thyme, leaves picked off and chopped

200g lentils, rinsed

400ml vegetable stock

Salt and ground black pepper

Oatcakes

260g pinhead oats

40g porridge oats

60g plain flour

½ tsp salt

¾ tsp baking powder

40g butter

1tbs olive oil

6–8 tbs hot water

Method

1. In a pot, boil lentils in the stock until cooked, approximately 20 minutes.

2. The mixture should be quite thick, set aside.

3. Sauté the chopped vegetables and garlic in the oil until soft, add the tomato puree, thyme and spices.

4. Mix the cooked vegetables into the lentil mix.

5. Season to taste, pour into a blender and whizz to a chunky pate, cover and chill.

Prep: 20 mins

Cook: 20 mins

For the oatcakes

Pre heat oven to 180C/160CFan/Gas4.

1. Mix together all the dry ingredients.

2. Melt the butter, mix with olive oil and add to the dry ingredients.

3. Then add hot water a little at a time until you have a sticky dough.

4. Turn dough out onto a surface generously dusted with oats and roll out until 1.5cm thick.

5. Cut with round cutter or into triangles and bake until golden brown.

Prep: under 10 minutes

Cook: 10 minutes

Cakes
. . .

Blueberry Coconut and Lemon Muffins

Makes 9 Muffins

Ingredients

225g gluten free self-raising flour

100g caster sugar

50g brown sugar

½ teaspoon gluten free baking powder

40g coconut, desiccated

1 peeled apple

½ punnet blueberries

30g Stork margarine (block)

2 tablespoons of sunflower oil

170ml cup soya milk

1 tablespoon lemon juice

Grated rind of a small lemon

Prep: Under 30 minutes

Cook: 15–20 minutes

Method

Preheat oven to 180C/160CFan/Gas4.
Use a 12 hole muffin tin and line nine with paper cases.

1. In a bowl combine flour, sugar, baking powder and coconut, add lemon rind, set aside.

2. In another bowl mix together the oil and Stork margarine followed by the milk and lemon juice.

3. Add wet ingredients to dry and finally grate in the apple. Stir until mixed, fold in the blueberries.

4. Divide into nine, add to the muffin tin and sprinkle with coconut. Bake for 15–20 minutes until the tops are golden brown, and the insides are dry: insert a cocktail stick to check.

Chocolate Fondant Cake
by Seumas MacInnes

Makes 12 slices – A Stunning cake so easy to make!

Ingredients

200g chocolate broken into pieces – preferably 70% cocoa

200g salted butter

250g caster sugar

6 medium free-range eggs

40g ground almonds

Prep: 20 minutes

Cook: 25 minutes

Method

Grease and line a 23cm (deep) sandwich pan while preheating the oven to 175C/155CFan/Gas3.

1. Put chocolate, butter and sugar into a plastic bowl and microwave on medium for 3 minutes. Stir until well mixed.

2. Beat or stir in eggs one at a time, then stir in ground almonds.

3. Scrape batter into pan and bake for 25 minutes. The centre should still be wobbly at this stage but it will firm up as it cools. Leave in the pan to lose the heat before turning out.

Serve

You can heat individual slices in a microwave for a few seconds before serving. Delicious with ice-cream and fresh raspberries!

Seumas MacInnes

Owner of Café Gandolfi, Seumas knows the hospitality industry from the bottom up, having started at Gandolfi in 1983 peeling potatoes and chopping cabbage. Seumas' family background on Barra has informed his approach to food – superb ingredients, cooked simply and served with care. A great philosophy, and something very close to my own heart. I have known Seumas for many years. We met through events in Glasgow, and we became friends. I've enjoyed many nights at his house. Seumas is a fantastic chef and host.

Dundee Cake
Makes one large cake

Ingredients

175g butter softened

3 tablespoons orange marmalade

75g glace cherries, halved

200g cup of currants

200g cup of sultanas

1 teaspoon ground mixed spice

3 medium free-range eggs

225g self-raising flour

25g ground almonds

175g soft light brown sugar

2 tablespoons of milk or whisky

40g blanched almonds to decorate

Prep: 35 minutes

Cook: 2 hours

Method

Preheat oven to 150C/130CFan/Gas2.
Grease and line a 20cm loose base deep cake tin.

1. Cream the butter and sugar in a food processor for 3–4 minutes.

2. Slowly add in one egg at a time, beat well after each addition, add the marmalade.

3. Add the flour, ground almonds and mixed spice to batter, mix slowly.

4. Add currants, sultanas and cherries.

5. Add milk or whisky and mix.

6. Pour into a lined dish, smooth the surface, cover the top with almonds and bake on the middle shelf of a moderate oven for 2 hours (test the cake by inserting a skewer into the centre, if it comes out clean the cake is ready).

7. Leave the cake to cool. Store in a cake tin and eat in 4–5 days.

Gluten and Dairy Free Carrot Cake

Makes a 900g loaf or 12 Mini Individual Cakes

Ingredients

150g light muscovado sugar

125ml sunflower oil

3 medium free-range eggs at room temperature

225g gluten free self-raising flour

½ tsp bicarbonate of soda

½ tsp baking powder

½ tsp ground mixed spice

½ tsp cinnamon

½ tsp ground ginger

250g carrots, grated

For the Icing

175g icing sugar

25g Stork margarine (block)

1 tbs soya milk

1 tsp sunflower oil

Prep: 30 minutes

Cook: 55 minutes for loaf or 30 minutes for individual

Method

Preheat the oven to 180C/160Fan/Gas4.

900g loaf tin lined with greaseproof paper or individual moulds.

1. Tip the sugar into a large mixing bowl. Whisk in the oil and add the eggs, one at a time.

2. Sift together the flour, bicarbonate of soda, baking powder, mixed spice, cinnamon and ginger and add this to the bowl, stirring well.

3. Stir in the grated carrots and mix all the ingredients evenly.

4. Spoon the mixture into prepared tin or moulds and bake for 50–55 minutes for loaf or 30 minutes for individual, until firm and springy in the centre and when a skewer inserted comes out clean.

5. Cool in tin for 10 minutes, then remove and cool completely on wire rack.

6. Make the icing: beat the margarine in a large bowl until really soft, add the icing sugar and other ingredients, beat until thick and creamy. Spread the icing on top.

Lemon Drizzle Cake

Makes a 900g loaf or 12 individual minis

Ingredients

110g butter

170g caster sugar

170g self-raising flour

Grated rind of a lemon

Juice of 1 lemon

2 medium free-range eggs

4 tablespoons milk

For the Icing

200g icing sugar

5 tablespoons lemon juice

Lemon zest from ½ lemon

Prep: Less than 30 minutes

Cook: 1 hour for loaf or 30 minutes for individual

Notes

This is easily made gluten and dairy free by substituting the butter for Stork margarine (block), the flour to gluten free flour, and the milk to soya

Method

Preheat oven to 180C/160CFan/Gas4

Line a 900g loaf tin with baking parchment, or individual moulds.

1. Beat the cake ingredients together until smooth, and then scrape the mix into the tin or individual moulds. Smooth the top.

2. Bake for about an hour, or 30 minutes for individual until a cocktail stick pushed into the centre comes out clean.

3. Leave to cool.

4. Use the juice of a lemon and drizzle on top.

5. For icing, mix icing sugar and lemon juice and grate in some lemon rind. When cakes are cool, drizzle over the icing.

Gluten Free Scones

Makes 12 scones

Ingredients

500g rice flour

4 teaspoons
xanthan gum

10 teaspoons gluten
free baking powder

8 tablespoons
icing sugar

100g butter (room
temperature)

600ml natural yoghurt

Prep: 15 minutes

Cook: 20–30 minutes

Method

Preheat oven to 200C/180CFan/Gas6.

1. Mix together the rice flour, xanthan gum, baking powder and sugar in a food processor.

2. Add in the butter to the flour.

3. Pour in the yoghurt and bring together into a soft dough.

4. Turn out the dough onto a floured surface and flatten with your hand to 2cm thick.

5. Use a no.70 cutter – push cutter straight down (as opposed to twisting) then lift straight out, gently push remaining dough together, knead very lightly, cut out more scones.

6. Place on a floured baking sheet.

7. Brush the tops of scones with water.

8. Bake in a preheated oven for 20 to 30 minutes.

Serve
With raspberry jam and whipped double cream.

Orange Thyme and Polenta Cake by Giovanna Eusebi

Makes one large cake

Ingredients

250g unsalted butter

250g caster sugar

4 large free-range eggs

140g polenta

200g plain flour

2 teaspoons baking powder

Zest and juice of 2 oranges

1 teaspoon finely chopped thyme

For the Glaze

100ml orange juice

100g caster sugar

Prep: Less than 30 minutes

Cook: 45 minutes

Method

Preheat oven 160C/140CFan/Gas3

Grease and line a 28cm cake tin.

1. Cream together butter and sugar.

2. Gradually add beaten egg.

3. Add all dry ingredients followed by orange juice and zest.

4. Put into the greased tin.

5. Bake for 45 minutes.

Take out of the oven and leave to cool.

Glaze

1. Boil together the orange juice and sugar. Reduce heat and simmer for 5 minutes.

2. Drizzle over cooled cake.

Giovanna Eusebi

Another East End girl, my mum used to shop in Eusebi's Deli and I got to know Giovanna through going into the shop with her. I was delighted when Giovanna decided to open her new restaurant in the West End, although it's not great for my diet! It has fast become a favourite for me. I am such a fan of Giovanna's attention to detail and menu selection. We love our chats about the business as well as talking about the old days, family and friends.

Sultana Scones

Makes about 12 – My Dad's favourite, he loves his lightly toasted.

Ingredients

225g self-raising flour

55g butter at room temperature

150ml milk

25g caster sugar

25g sultanas

A pinch of salt

1 medium free-range egg beaten

Prep: Less than 30 minutes

Cook: 12–15 minutes

Method

Preheat the oven to 220C/200CFan/Gas7.
Prepare a baking sheet, greased.

1. Sift the flour into a bowl and rub the butter into it rapidly, using your fingertips.

2. Next stir in the sugar and salt, then take a knife and use it to mix in the milk, little by little

3. Now flour your hands and knead the mixture to a soft dough – adding a drop more milk if it feels dry.

4. Turn the dough out on to a floured board and roll out to a thickness of no less than 2cm using a floured rolling pin. Take a 5cm pastry cutter and place it on the dough and cut through. After you have cut out the scones, knead the remaining dough and repeat till you have used it all.

5. Place the scones on the greased sheet, brush the top with beaten egg and bake near the top of the oven for 12–15 minutes. Cool on a wire rack.

6. Serve with jam and clotted cream.

Stem Ginger Cake
by Andrew Fairlie

Makes one large cake

Ingredients

230g self-raising flour

1 tablespoon bicarbonate of soda

1 tablespoon powdered ginger

1 tablespoon powdered cinnamon

1 tablespoon powdered all spice

110g unsalted butter, diced

110g black treacle

110g golden syrup

110g dark brown sugar

280ml milk

45g stem ginger from a jar, chopped

1 medium free-range egg, beaten

Prep: 25 minutes

Cook: 50 minutes

Method

Preheat oven to 180C/160CFan/Gas 4.
Grease and line a 900g loaf tin.

1. Sift the flour, bicarbonate of soda and spices into a bowl, add the diced butter and rub till the texture resembles fine breadcrumbs.

2. Melt the treacle and syrup in a saucepan and leave to cool to room temperature.

3. In a separate pan melt the sugar in the milk, add the ginger, and again leave to cool to room temperature.

4. Mix the milk into the flour mix, and then add the treacle followed by the egg.

5. Pour the mix into the prepared loaf tin and bake in the oven for 45 to 50 minutes.

6. Leave to rest for 10 minutes, remove from the tin and cool on a wire rack.

Serve

A family favourite and easy to make, it can be topped with an orange icing or eaten at room temperature from the oven.

Andrew Fairlie

Andrew is a renowned Scottish chef and patron of the eponymous Restaurant Andrew Fairlie within the world-famous Gleneagles Hotel and Resort at Auchterarder in Perthshire, the only two Michelin star restaurant in Scotland. I met Andrew when he worked at One Devonshire Gardens, through a friend of a friend, and was lucky enough to be invited to Andrew's opening night at Gleneagles. I love my visits and always enjoy sampling his amazing food.

Chocolate Orange Cake
Makes one large cake

Ingredients

100g unsalted butter plus some extra

50g cocoa powder

90ml boiling water

3 large free-range eggs

4 tablespoons milk

175g self-rising flour

1 tsp baking powder

300g caster sugar

Zest of 1 orange finely grated

For the icing and filling

200g dark chocolate, broken into small pieces

200g double cream

For decoration

A bag of Terry's mini chocolate oranges

Prep: Under 30 minutes
Cook: 20–25 minutes

Notes

You need to make your icing first for this cake

Method

Preheat oven to 180C/160CFan/Gas4.
Grease 2x20cm round sandwich tins and line the bases with baking paper.

1. Make the icing: put the chocolate and cream in a bowl, then stand the bowl in a pan of simmering water (don't let the bowl touch the sides) until chocolate melts, stirring occasionally. Cool and put in fridge until it thickens to a spreading consistency.

2. To make the sponges, put the cocoa and boiling water into a free standing mixer and mix to a paste.

3. Add the remaining ingredients and beat again until combined. Be careful not to over-mix.

4. Divide the sponge mixture evenly between the prepared tins.

5. Bake in a preheated oven for 20–25 minutes until the sponges are well risen and shrinking away from the sides of the tins. Remove the sponges from the oven, turn out on to a cooling rack and leave to cool.

6. To finish, spread the top of one sponge with half the icing and put the other sponge on top.

7. Pipe a little icing on the top sponge, then pipe the top of the cake with the remainder of the icing and scatter the mini chocolate oranges.

Victoria Sponge

Makes one large cake

Ingredients

For the sponge

6 medium free-range eggs

300g self-raising flour

300g caster sugar

300g butter

1 teaspoon baking powder

3 tablespoons milk

For the filling

170g raspberry jam

300g double cream, whipped

Icing sugar

Optional: fruit to decorate

Prep: less than 30 minutes

Cook: 30 minutes

Method

Preheat oven to 190C/170CFan/Gas5.

Grease and line three 20cm baking tins with non-stick baking paper.

1. Place all the ingredients in a large bowl and beat until you have a smooth soft batter.

2. Put the mixture in the tins, smooth the surface with a spatula or back of a spoon, then bake for 30 minutes. You know it's baked if it springs back when pressed.

3. Turn out on to a rack and leave to cool.

4. Spread jam over the bottom of one of the sponges, pipe the cream over the jam, sandwich the second sponge on top and repeat with the third sponge.

5. Sprinkle with icing sugar and to make it really special, top with whipped cream and fruit before serving.

Puddings
and desserts

■ ■ ■

Apple Tart Tatin
by Gary Maclean

Using a 22–23cm pan, Serves 4–6

Ingredients

4 apples, peeled, cut in half length ways and cored (Cox and Braeburn)

50g caster sugar

50g unsalted butter

1 circle puff pastry – 1cm wider than the pan

Prep: 30 minutes

Cook: 35 minutes

Method

Insert Preheat oven to 220C/200CFan/Gas8

1. Sprinkle the sugar on the bottom of a heavy based, oven proof frying pan and dot the softened butter on top of the sugar.

2. Place the apples on top with the rounded side down into the butter and the sugar.

3. Start the caramelization process over a medium-high heat. As the caramel starts to color and darken, reduce the heat with every shade until the finishing shade of a golden light mahogany is achieved. This will take approximately 12–15 minutes. Remove from the heat and allow to cool. If the caramel is made without the apples, the apples are likely to be undercooked at the end resulting in very little flavour in the end result.

4. Once the apples and caramel have cooled, place the puff pastry on top and tuck the edges around and under the apples, meeting the pastry underneath. Cook the tart in the oven for about 10 minutes then reduce the heat to 200C/180CFan/Gas6 and cook for a further 20 minutes.

5. Remove from the oven and allow to stand for at least 20 minutes. Do not turn out immediately. After 20 minutes gently reheat the tart until it loosens.

Gary Maclean

A lecturer at City of Glasgow College and a very worthy winner of Masterchef 2016. I met Gary through helping with the Rotary Club of Glasgow Young Chef of the Year competition. I always enjoy meeting up with him at the annual prize-giving ceremony for students.

Chocolate Eclairs
Makes approx 12-15

Ingredients

Choux pastry

125ml water

50g unsalted butter
(extra butter for
greasing)

100g plain flour

3 medium free-range
eggs, beaten

For filling and topping

150g chocolate

100ml cream for
chocolate

300ml cream

Prep: 30 – 40 minutes

Cook: 30 – 40 minutes

Method

Preheat the oven 220C/200CFan/Gas7.

1. Add water to a small saucepan and place butter in, melt over a low heat and bring to the boil.

2. Remove from the heat and stir in the flour.

3. Return to the heat, stirring until mixture forms a ball in the middle of the pan.

4. Remove from the heat and allow to cool.

5. Add eggs one at a time and thoroughly beat the mixture with a wooden spoon. The mixture will become slippery and soft when the egg is added, beat until it returns to a firmer consistency.

6. Grease a baking tray, run under the cold tap for a second, leaving a film of water on the tray.

7. Place the choux paste into a piping bag with a 1cm nozzle.

8. Pipe the mixture on to the greased tray into 7cm lengths and bake in oven for 20 minutes.

9. Remove from the oven, immediately put on to a cooling rack and slice along one side of every eclair (this will prevent them collapsing and will become the filling entry for the cream).

10. Allow to cool.

11. Melt chocolate and cream in a Bain-Marie, set aside to cool slightly.

12. Whip cream up to firm consistency and then pipe into your cooled eclairs.

13. Spoon some chocolate over each and allow the chocolate to set.

Clootie Dumpling

Serve thick Slices, with custard and perhaps a small glass of whisky.

Ingredients

200g plain white flour
plus 25g for sprinkling

1 tsp bicarbonate of soda

1 tsp ground mixed spice

1 tsp ground cinnamon

1 tsp ground ginger

¼ tsp freshly ground
sea salt

175g caster sugar
plus 1 tablespoon for
sprinkling

100g shredded suet

100g sultanas

85g currants

85g chopped stoned dates

50g muscatel raisins

1 apple coarsely grated

1 tbs black treacle

1 medium
free-range egg

About 150ml buttermilk

Prep: 30 minutes
to 1 hour

Cook: 4 hours

Notes

If using vegetable suet,
suitable for vegetarians

Method

1. Sift the flour, bicarbonate of soda, spices and salt into a bowl and stir in the sugar, suet, dried fruits and grated apple.

2. Mix black treacle with egg and enough of the buttermilk to give a soft mixture with a cake-like dropping consistency when mixed into the dry ingredients.

3. Dip a large piece of muslin, like an old pillowcase, a pudding cloth or tea towel into boiling water, remove it and squeeze out excess water. Lay it out on a surface and, in the centre, sprinkle the extra flour and sugar in a 30cm circle.

4. Spoon the pudding mixture on top, carefully gather up the corners of the cloth to shape the pudding mix into a sphere and tie securely with string. Leave a little room for the pudding to expand.

5. Rest a heatproof plate in the base of a large pan as a trivet, so that it is not in direct contact with the heat, and place the pudding on the plate, knotted side up. Pour in enough water almost to cover the pudding, cover with a tight fitting lid and simmer gently for about 4 hrs. Take a look every now and then to check the water level and top it up if necessary.

6. Preheat the oven to 180C/160CFan/Gas 4.

7. Lift the pudding out of the pan and dip it briefly in a bowl of cold water – this will ensure that the outside of the pudding doesn't stick – unwrap the pudding and transfer it to an ovenproof serving plate.

8. Slide it into the oven and leave for 15 minutes, until the outside of the pudding has dried off and is dark and glossy. Allow to cool and store in an airtight container for up to seven days.

Lemon Meringue Pie

Makes one large pie

Ingredients

For the pastry:

225g plain flour, plus a little extra for rolling out

175g butter, cubed

45g icing sugar

1 large free-range egg yolk, beaten (use the white for meringue)

For the filling:

3 heaped tablespoons cornflour

3 large lemons, grated lemon zest and juice approx. 125ml

200ml cold water

100g caster sugar

3 free-range egg yolks and 1 whole egg

85g butter, cut into pieces

For the meringue:

4 free-range egg whites (1 from pastry and 3 from filling)

200g caster sugar

2 teaspoons cornflour

Method

Pre heat oven to 180C/160CFan/Gas4.
23cm loose bottom flan tin.

Pastry

1. Put the flour, butter, icing sugar, 1 tablespoon water and egg yolk into a food processor, use the pulse button and process until the mix starts to bind, do not overwork the mixture.

2. Tip the pastry on to a lightly floured surface, gather together until smooth and roll out to a 3mm thickness. Transfer pastry to a 23cm loose bottom flan tin, cover in cling film and let it rest in the fridge for 30 minutes to 1 hour.

3. Take pastry out of fridge; trim excess, press the top edge so it stands higher than the top of the tin, it needs to stand tall for the filling. Line the pastry case with parchment paper and fill with baking beans.

4. Place tin on a baking sheet and bake in the preheated oven for about 15 minutes, then remove beans and parchment paper and cook again for 5 minutes.

5. Remove the pastry case and turn down heat to 170C/150Fan/Gas3.

Filling

1. Mix the cornflour, sugar and lemon zest in a bowl. Strain the lemon juice and stir in gradually to the cornflour, to make a smooth paste.

2. Put the water in a pan, bring to the boil, add the cornflour paste to the hot water and stir constantly over a medium heat until the mixture is thick and smooth. Take off the heat, beat in the butter until melted. Beat in the egg yolks and whole egg, stir and return to the heat, keep stirring constantly for a few minutes, until the mixture thickens, take off the heat.

Continued overleaf

Meringue Mix

Pre heat oven to 190C/170CFan/Gas5.

1. For the meringue, in a squeaky clean bowl, whisk the egg whites in a free standing mixer until they form soft peaks.

2. Add a tablespoon of caster sugar at a time until it is all incorporated, rub some mixture between your fingers to check there is no trace of sugar granules, then add the cornflour and whisk again.

3. Spoon the meringue on top of the pie, starting at the edge of the pastry, then fill the middle of the pie and create swirls on the top of the meringue.

4. Bake in the oven for 20 minutes until meringue is crisp and lightly coloured. Let the pie cool for 30 minutes, if you are serving warm.

Prep: 30 mins to 1 hour

Cook: 45 mins to 1 hour

Meringues
Makes about 14 shells

Ingredients

4 medium free-range egg whites at room temperature

225g caster sugar

Pinch of salt

Pink food colouring

For the filling

Double cream

Fruit

Prep: 15 minutes

Cook: 1 hour plus cooling

Method

Preheat the oven to 150C/130CFan/Gas2.

Lightly oil two baking sheets and line with baking parchment.

1. Place the egg whites in a large dry, clean grease free bowl and whisk into soft peaks. (Do not get any yolk in to bowl or meringues will not work).

2. To test for right consistency, tip the bowl at an angle – if the mixture doesn't slide out, it's ready. It should also look slightly dry. Take care not to over beat or the whites will collapse.

3. Whisk in the sugar, about one tablespoon at a time, making sure that you whisk thoroughly after each addition. When all the sugar is whisked in, the mixture should be smooth, thick and glossy and form stiff sharp peaks when the beaters are lifted out.

4. Rub a small amount of the meringue mix between your fingers, to make sure there is no trace of sugar granules.

5. Place a dessertspoonful of the mixture slightly apart on the baking sheets. For the ripple colour effect, dip a wooden or metal skewer into the food colouring and swirl through each meringue.

6. Place in the oven, reduce the heat to 140C/120CFan/Gas1 and bake for 1 hour.

7. Turn off the heat and leave in the oven to cool.

8. Whip cream until it forms soft peaks, then use to sandwich pairs of meringues together. Decorate with fruit.

Once filled, the meringues should be eaten on the same day. Unfilled meringues should be stored in an airtight tin for 4 – 5 days.

Sticky Toffee Pudding
by Ryan James

Ingredients

175g self-raising flour

175g caster sugar

175g pitted
chopped dates

2 medium
free-range eggs

50g butter

1 teaspoon vanilla
extract

1 teaspoon bicarbonate
of soda

For the toffee sauce

100g butter

100g muscovado sugar

150ml double cream

Prep: less than 30
minutes

Cook: 40–45 minutes

Method

Preheat oven to 190C/170C/Gas5.
Grease a 20cm square cake tin with butter.

1. Place the dates and 300ml of water in a saucepan and bring to the boil, add the bicarbonate of soda.

2. In a freestanding mixer, cream the butter and sugar together, gradually add eggs and vanilla, add the flour and stir in the date mixture.

3. Pour into the cake tin and bake for 40–45 minutes.

Toffee Sauce

1. Put all ingredients into a pan and stir over a low heat until sugar has dissolved and the butter has melted.

2. Bring to the boil, stirring for a minute.

Serve

Cut cake into squares, drizzle with sauce and serve with cream or ice cream.

Ryan James

Current Chair of Glasgow Restauranteurs Association (GRA) and owner of Two Fat Ladies, Ryan is a strong supporter of the hospitality sector. He is always keen to get involved in new and innovative projects to help promote our great city of Glasgow and it's wonderful to have him as Chair of GRA.

Strawberry Cheesecake
Makes one large cake

Ingredients

For the base

400g digestive biscuits

200g melted butter

For the filling

450g softened cream cheese

10tbs caster sugar

400ml double cream, whipped

Topping

1 punnet of strawberries for decorating

1 punnet of strawberries for sauce

25g icing sugar

1 teaspoon water

Prep: At least 30 minutes

Method

Grease and line a 23cm loose bottom cake tin with baking parchment.

1. To make the base, put the biscuits in a bowl and crush with a rolling pin, add the melted butter. Mix thoroughly until the crumbs are completely coated.

2. Tip the base mix into the prepared tin and press firmly down into the base to create an even layer. Chill in the fridge for at least 30 minutes.

3. To make the filling, place the soft cheese and icing sugar into a bowl and beat with an electric mixer until smooth. Fold in the whipped cream.

4. Spoon the mixture onto the biscuit base, smooth the top of the cheesecake down with the back of a dessert spoon and leave to set in the refrigerator for 2 hours, or ideally overnight.

5. To unmould, place the base on top of a can and gradually pull the sides down, slip the cake onto a serving plate.

6. To make strawberry sauce, put one punnet of strawberries, icing sugar and water into a blender, then sieve.

7. Once the cheesecake has set, garnish with another punnet of strawberries sliced, and pour over the puree.

Tray bakes and biscuits
...

Caramel Shortcake

Makes 9

Ingredients

For the shortbread

225g plain flour

75g caster sugar

175g butter, cold, cut into cubes

For the caramel

50g caster sugar

150g butter, cut up into several pieces (to make salted caramel add 1 teaspoon rock salt and salted butter)

397g can condensed milk

100g golden syrup

For the topping

350g dark chocolate (70% cocoa solids) you can use a mix of dark and milk chocolate

Prep: 30 minutes plus chilling

Cook: 30 minutes to 1 hour

Method

Preheat oven to 160C/140C/Gas3.
Lightly grease and line a 23cm square tin.

1. To make the shortbread, put the flour and butter in a food processor, and pulse until the mixture resembles fine breadcrumbs. Add caster sugar and pulse again until combined. Take out and knead the mixture together until it forms a dough, then press into the base of the prepared tin. Prick the shortbread lightly with a fork and bake in the preheated oven for about 30 minutes or until firm to the touch and very lightly browned. Cool in the tin.

2. To make the caramel, put the butter, sugar, golden syrup and condensed milk into a pan and heat on medium-high, stirring gently, until the sugar has dissolved. Watch it closely as you stir, if you start to see slivers of brown where it has stuck to the bottom of the pan, stir them vigorously and turn the heat down to low-medium. Simmer gently until it is a deep golden brown (if you want salted caramel add your salt now).

3. Pour the caramel over the shortbread base and spread it with a knife and leave to cool for at least an hour.

4. For the topping, melt the chocolate slowly in a bowl over a pan of hot water. Pour over the cold caramel, spread gently with a knife, and leave to set. Cut into squares.

Gluten Free or not Chocolate Brownies

Makes 12

Ingredients

250g unsalted butter

350g best quality dark chocolate (70% cocoa solids)

3 large free-range eggs

250g dark brown sugar

100g gluten free plain flour, sifted

1 teaspoon gluten free baking powder

Prep: 20 minutes

Cook: 25 minutes

Notes

If you don't want our delicious gluten free option, change to plain flour and baking power

Method

Preheat the oven to 180C/160CFan/Gas3.
Lightly grease and line 22cm square tin.

1. Melt the chocolate and butter in a heatproof bowl over a pan of simmering water, and then cool.

2. Whisk the eggs and sugar together for 3–4 minutes until pale, smooth and fluffy.

3. Fold in the chocolate mixture to the egg mixture.

4. Add the flour and baking powder into the mixture and gently stir to mix.

5. Pour the mixture into the tin and smooth out.

6. Place on the middle shelf of the oven and bake for 25 minutes until the surface is set. It is cooked when it just starts to crack on the top.

7. The top should be dried to a paler brown speckle, but the middle still dark and dense and gooey. You do need to keep alert, keep checking. The difference between gungy brownies and dry brownies is only a few minutes, they will continue to cook while they cool.

8. Cool in the tin. Chill in the fridge.

9. Slice into squares and store in a tin or container in the fridge.

10. Dust with cocoa powder or icing sugar and add a dollop of cream.

Paradise Slice

Makes 12-16

Ingredients

Pastry

227g plain flour, sifted

113g butter, cut into cubes

28g caster sugar

1 medium free-range egg

Filling

200g raspberry jam

170g caster sugar

57g butter, softened

2 small free-range eggs, beaten

113g desiccated coconut

113g sultanas

57g glace cherries, halved

Prep: 20 minutes plus resting

Cook: 40 minutes

Method

1. First make the pastry: place the flour, butter and sugar in a food processor and process until the mixture resembles breadcrumbs.

2. Add the egg through the feeder tube and process until combined.

3. Wrap in cling film and chill for I hour.

4. Roll out the pastry to fit a lightly buttered 25 x 18cm baking tin.

5. Prick all over.

6. Preheat the oven to 190C/170Fan/Gas5.

7. Line the pastry with foil, fill with baking beans and bake 'blind' for 15 minutes.

8. Remove the foil and beans and cook the pastry for a further 10 minutes.

9. Allow to cool. Reduce the oven to 180C/160CFan/Gas4.

10. Once the base is cool, spread with jam.

11. Cream together the sugar and butter, then beat in the eggs.

12. Fold in the coconut, sultanas and cherries and combine well.

13. Pour over the jam, ensuring the base is evenly covered.

14. Bake in the oven for about 30 minutes, or until golden brown and set.

15. Allow to cool in the tin for about 20 minutes, and then cut into squares with a sharp knife.

The Three Chimneys Shortbread by Shirley Spear

Makes up to 24 biscuits

Ingredients

250g Scottish salted butter, plus a small amount for greasing the baking trays

125g caster sugar, plus extra for sprinkling on the cooked shortbread

250g plain flour, plus extra for rolling and cutting

125g white rice flour

Prep: less than 30 minutes

Cook: 20 minutes

Method

Preheat the oven to 190C/170CFan/Gas5.
Lightly grease two baking trays, using the butter wrapping.

1. Cream together the butter and caster sugar with a wooden spoon until light and fluffy.

2. Sieve together the plain flour and rice flour and add to the butter mixture.

3. Mix together well with a wooden spoon and then, using clean fingers, gather the mixture together into a ball of dough. This may seem a little bit dry at first, but it will come together.

4. Sprinkle some flour on a clean work surface or board. Gently knead the dough together until it is soft and pliable in the warmth of your hands.

5. Roll out the dough to the thickness of a one pound coin. Cut the biscuit shapes and lift, using a palette knife, on to the greased baking trays.

6. Prick the biscuits with a fork and place the trays in the oven to bake for 15–20 minutes until very light golden brown.

7. Remove from the oven and sprinkle with caster sugar while still warm. Leave to cool slightly and carefully lift the biscuits on to a wire tray to cool completely. They will continue to crisp-up as they get cold.

8. Store in an airtight tin between layers of non-stick parchment paper, for one or two weeks at most.

Shirley Spear

Shirley and her husband Eddie led the way in restoring pride amongst Scottish chefs in our nation's culinary heritage. This is evident at their own restaurant, The Three Chimneys, on the Isle of Skye. Shirley is one of my inspirations.

Sinful Slice

Makes 16 – Robyn and Ryan's favourite!

Ingredients

425g digestive biscuits

170g milk chocolate broken into pieces

85g butter

170g Golden Syrup

110g cherries, quartered

85g sultanas

55g nuts

400g chocolate for topping

white chocolate to decorate

Prep: less than 30 minutes

Cook: no cooking

Method

1. Crush the biscuits roughly.

2. Put the chocolate, butter and Golden Syrup in a bowl and melt in microwave, stir to mix.

3. Mix the remaining ingredients.

4. Lightly grease and line a swiss roll tin 33x23, and press the mixture in firmly and evenly.

5. Melt the chocolate and cover.

6. Melt the white chocolate and drizzle over.

7. Chill in the fridge 1–2 hours, and cut into squares.

Empire Biscuits

Makes 8 biscuits – Peter and Lisa's absolute favourite!

Ingredients

225g plain flour, sifted

150g butter

75g caster sugar

Raspberry jam for filling

For the topping

Glacé cherries, halved

200g icing sugar

Water (a teaspoon at a time)

Prep: 10 minutes

Cook: 8–10 minutes

Notes

If you want to make vegan substitute butter for Stork margarine block.

Method

Preheat oven to 180C/160CFan/Gas4.

1. Place flour, sugar and butter in a free standing machine.

2. Mix on the lowest setting with a flat beater.

3. The mixture will go through a breadcrumb consistency, then will form a dough.

4. Bring all of the dough together, taking care not to knead too much or you will lose the short consistency.

5. Roll the dough out to 5mm thickness.

6. Cut into circles using a pastry cutter.

7. Line baking trays with baking parchment.

8. Bake in oven for 8–10 minutes until lightly golden.

9. Let the biscuits cool.

10. Put a teaspoon of jam on to a biscuit, spread to near the edge, then top with a second biscuit, repeat until all biscuits are used up.

11. Mix together icing sugar and a teaspoon of water at a time, to make a spreadable icing.

12. Use a warm knife to spread.

13. Top each biscuit with a half a glacé cherry.

Oatmeal Raisin Cookies

Makes approx 12 – 15

Ingredients

256g self-raising flour

½ teaspoon baking powder

1 teaspoon salt

227g Stork margarine (block) softened

128g caster sugar

220g dark brown sugar

1 tablespoon lemon juice

2 teaspoons vanilla essence

255g oats (not instant)

225g raisins

Prep: 10–15 minutes
Cook: 10–15 minutes

Method

Preheat oven to 180C/160CFan/Gas4.
Baking sheet, sprayed with spray oil.

1. Whisk flour, baking power and salt, set aside.

2. Combine margarine, caster sugar, dark brown sugar, lemon juice and vanilla essence with hand mixer.

3. To cream, increase speed to high and beat until fluffy and the colour lightens.

4. Stir the flour mixture into the creamed mixture until no flour is visible. Don't overmix.

5. Now add the oats and raisins, stir in to incorporate.

6. Take a heaped tablespoon of dough and roll in to balls, place well apart onto the baking sheet.

7. Bake for 10–15 minutes on centre rack until golden.

8. Remove from the oven. Let cookies sit on baking sheet for 2 minutes before transferring to a wire rack to cool.

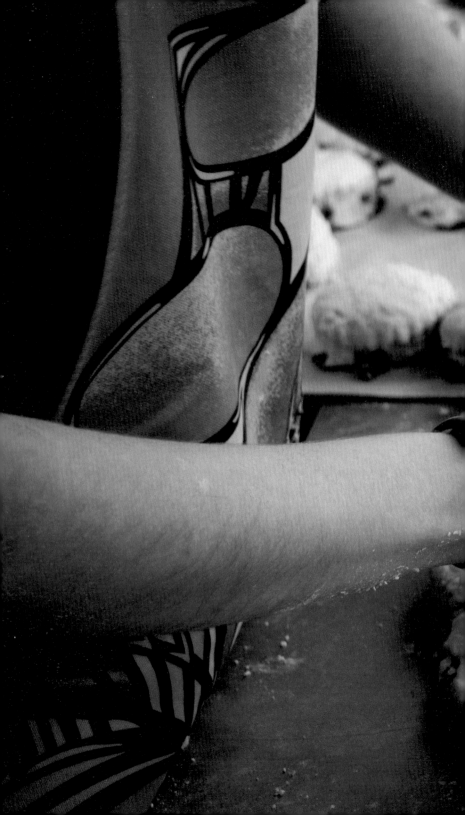

Breads
...

Banana Bread
by Drew Murray

Ingredients

140g butter

140g caster sugar

140g self-raising flour

2 large free-range egg

1 teaspoon baking powder

2 ripe bananas, mashed

Prep: 10 minutes

Cook: 50 minutes

Method

Preheat oven 180C/160CFan/Gas4.
Grease and line a 900g loaf tin.

1. Cream butter and sugar until light and fluffy.

2. Beat in the eggs, one at a time.

3. Fold in sieved flour.

4. Mash the bananas (no lumps) and add the baking powder, they will froth up.

5. Add banana mixture to other mixture.

6. Place in loaf tin and bake for approximately 50 minutes.

7. Cool in the tin for 10 minutes, then remove to a wire rack.

Drew Murray

Drew is a Lecturer at John Wheatley College and has been a good friend to me and to the Willow Tea Rooms over the last 25 years. He is so good at recommending students to me who he knows will be hard-working members of the team. Over the years, I have stolen lots of his recipes, he has taught me a lot, and we have worked together in the kitchen on a number of occasions.

Potato Scones
by Craig McPhie

Ingredients

225g cooked mashed
potatoes

½ teaspoon salt

15g melted butter

65g soft plain flour

Prep: 15 minutes

Cook: 10–15 minutes

Method

1. Peel and boil potatoes in salted water until tender, drain.

2. Take cooked potato and mash well.

3. Add the salt, melted butter and mix well until all ingredients have cleared.

4. Add flour and mix through until clear.

5. Pin out the dough, using a dusting of flour to stop sticking to pin or table, to a thickness of 5mm or thicker if you prefer.

6. Cut into the required shapes and place on hot plate or griddle with a very hot temperature, 250C (Do not oil the plate as it will just burn).

7. Cook for approximately 4 minutes before turning when the base becomes a light golden colour.

8. Turn the potato scone over and cook for a further 3 minutes or until it becomes light golden in colour.

Craig McPhie

Craig, and his dad Jim, from McPhies Craft Bakers, were my local bakers when we lived in the East End. Craig has helped me source the traditional, home-baked cakes I knew I wanted to serve. Over the years we have worked together and have become good friends. I'm delighted that Craig is following in his dad's footsteps as President of the Scottish Bakers' Association – an honour well deserved.

Granny's Irish Soda Bread
by Lorraine McIntosh

Ingredients

170g self-raising wholemeal flour

170g plain flour

½ teaspoon salt

½ teaspoon bicarbonate of soda

290ml buttermilk

Prep: 30 minutes

Cook: 30 minutes

Method

Preheat oven to 200C/180CFan/Gas6.

1. Mix the flour, bicarbonate of soda and salt in a large mixing bowl and stir (I never sift the flour, but some do).

2. Make a well in the middle and pour in your buttermilk, mixing it quickly with a fork until it forms a soft dough. If the dough feels too stiff add a little drop of milk to soften it – but don't get it too wet.

3. Turn it out onto a lightly floured surface and knead gently.

4. Form into a round shape and place it on a lightly floured baking sheet. Cut a criss-cross on the top.

5. Bake for 30 minutes until the loaf sounds empty when you tap.

6. Remove from oven and cool on a wire rack.

Before it gets completely cool, cut a large slice and spread thickly with some salted butter.

Lorraine McIntosh

Lorraine is best known as a vocalist with one of my favourite Scottish bands, Deacon Blue. However, it was through the great friendship of my daughter, Robyn, and Lorraine's daughter, Emer, that David and I became family friends with Ricky and Lorraine.

Gingerbread

Ingredients

170g treacle

85g brown sugar

85g Stork margarine (block)

1 tablespoon lemon juice

255g self-raising flour

½ teaspoon baking powder

1 grated apple

1 teaspoon mixed spice

½ teaspoon ground ginger

½ teaspoon cinnamon

For the topping

200g icing sugar

Cold water

Prep: 15–20 minutes

Cook: 50–55 minutes

Method

Preheat oven to 180C/160CFan/Gas4.
Grease and line 900g loaf tin.

1. In a bowl, mix together the flour, baking powder and spices.

2. In a pan place the syrup, treacle, margarine and sugar and dissolve on a low heat until the mixture has melted together.

3. Finely grate the apple into the flour mix, then add the melted ingredients. Next mix in the lemon juice.

4. When everything is combined, pour into loaf tin and bake for 50–55 minutes until a skewer comes out of the centre dry.

To Ice

Mix icing sugar with a teaspoon of water at a time, until spreading consistency, and leave to firm.

Confectionery

...

Coconut Ice Squares

Ingredients

250g condensed milk

275g icing sugar

200g desiccated coconut

50g pistachio nuts, roughly chopped

¾ tsp cardamom pods, crushed

Pink food colouring

Prep: 15 minutes, plus chilling

Method

Grease and line a 23cm tin.

1. Mix the condensed milk and icing sugar in a bowl until quite stiff and add in the coconut. Mix until well combined.

2. Split the mix into two bowls: in one bowl add the cardamom and chopped nuts, and in the other bowl add the pink food colouring till desired colour is reached.

3. Press the first mixture into the tin, press down hard to smooth, then add the second mix on top, smooth and press until it is even.

4. Leave to chill for 3 hours, cut into bite-sized pieces.

Tip: use your hands to mix the coconut into the sugar mix.

Whisky Tablet

Ingredients

500ml milk

225g butter plus extra
to grease

1.8kg caster sugar

½ teaspoon salt

397g condensed milk

45ml whisky

Prep: under 20 minutes

Cook: 30–40 minutes

Method

Grease a 25x35cm Swiss roll tin.

1. Place the milk and butter in a heavy based saucepan on a low heat and melt the butter.

2. Add the sugar and salt and bring to the boil, stirring all the time.

3. Once the mixture is boiling, add the condensed milk and boil for 20 minutes. Again keep stirring to avoid it sticking or burning. You will know when it is ready when it thickens and the colour changes, becoming a light a light tan colour.

4. Take off the heat and beat vigorously for 5–10 minutes, add the whisky. It will gradually become grainy. Just continue beating and scraping the sides of the pan and incorporating the crystals into the mixture.

5. Pour into Swiss roll tin and allow it to set, then score with a sharp knife while still soft. Once it has cooled, after about 20 minutes, cut into small squares. The texture is crumbly and melts in the mouth.

Once properly cold, the tablet will keep for weeks in an airtight box.

I promise you it will never last that long!

American Conversion Table

Spoons, Cups and Liquid

Spoons & Cups	ml
¼ teaspoon	1.25ml
½ teaspoon	2.5ml
1 teaspoon	5ml
1 tablespoon	15ml
¼ cup	60ml
⅓ cup	80ml
½ cup	125ml
1 cup	250ml

Temperature

Gas Mark	°C	°F
1	140°C	275°F
2	150°C	300°F
3	170°C	325°F
4	180°C	350°F
5	190°C	375°F
6	200°C	400°F
7	220°C	425°F
8	230°C	450°F
9	240°C	475°F

American Cups to Grams

Ingredients	Grams
1 cup butter	225g
1 stick butter	113g
1 cup flour	125g
1 cup white sugar	225g
1 cup brown sugar	200g
1 cup icing sugar	125g
1 cup raisins/sultanas	200g
1 cup currants	150g
1 cup ground almonds	110g
1 cup syrup	350g
1 cup rice (uncooked)	200g

Common Ingredients / Tool Names

Caster sugar	Superfine sugar
Icing sugar	Powdered sugar
Plain flour	All-purpose
Marzipan	Almond paste
Self-raising flour	Self-rising flour
Sultanas	Golden raisins
Cling film	Plastic wrap
Cupcake cases	Paper liners

Acknowledgements

This book would not have been possible without the help and support of so many people.

First of all, my family. My husband David, daughter Robyn and son Ryan, who have been with me all the way on this project. The parts they enjoyed most, of course, were the tasting sessions! What could be better than sampling 40 different tasty treats and savouries – even though I said on many occasions you have had this before – the answer was always, "but we need to keep up the quality checking". More importantly was the love and encouragement they gave me to keep going when deadlines were near, and how willing they all were to help out with whatever was needed – this is something that was so important to me and makes this book worthwhile – it is dedicated to them and all the years they have lived through the Willow experience with me.

My dad, George, and brother, Marcus, have always been very supportive in everything I do. My dad is so proud being able to tell our story to his friends, many of whom enjoy visiting him for a bit of homemade cake, although he has been known to forget to tell them it is there – particularly when there are only a couple of bits left.

Over the years, I have added to my family! I have now an adopted sister... my Business Manager, Sheila Proctor. Sheila joined me at the Willow Tea Rooms in 2008 and has in that time became a lifelong friend – nothing is too much trouble and she supports me in all I do without a moment's hesitation.

I am grateful for the help and support from my friends, 'The Bakers' Dozen'. When I mentioned what I was doing and was perhaps looking for a recipe or two, there was not a moment's hesitation, they were all keen to be involved and loved the idea of being part of the Willow story. So, to AJ, Andrew, Archie, Craig, Drew, Gary, Giovanna, Greg, Kirsty, Lorraine, Ryan, Seumas and Shirley a massive thank you. You will never know how much it means to me that you all said yes.

For helping me get the book onto the shelves, I am indebted to two people, Adrian Searle and Lisa Watt. Nothing was a bother, no matter how many times I said, "is it okay if I change…" Thank you for being so patient and for helping me realise this dream.

The success of the Willow Tea Rooms is down to a fantastic team effort. Helping me throughout the project has been my Tea Room Manager, Joanne McNamee, who willingly turned her hand to whatever was needed as we worked on the book's development. My staff are always willing to get involved in anything new, their support is so important to me. But I do need to single out a couple of people for a special mention – Anna Howard and Amy Robertson. Anna and Amy work tirelessly producing all the delicious cakes and scones and who have both been involved with me in producing all the great recipes for my book – thank you both for all your hard work.

Lastly, a big thank you to each and every single customer who has come through our doors. My business would not be the success it is if it was not for you. When I opened the doors of the Willow Tea Rooms, 34 years ago, I would never have believed that so many of my customers would become my friends – something that fills me with pride every day. I hope you enjoy reading our story and more importantly making the delicious cakes, scones and savouries.

Love
Anne xx

Appendix – Types of tea

Indian

Assam	A strong tea with a malty flavour, best served with milk not lemon.
Darjeeling	Regarded as the finest and most distinctive of Indian teas, has a delicate Muscatel flavour.
Mysore	A mild, light coloured tea with a fruity flavour.
Ceylon	Medium strength with a mellow nutty flavour.
Kenya	Similar to Ceylon and often used for blending.
English Breakfast	Made from small leaf teas of India and Ceylon, rich and strong, astringent in flavour, the perfect tea to wake you up in the morning.

China

Keemun	A tea from North China, yellow and smooth, pale straw in colour with a 'fragrance like an orchid'.
Ching Wo	Delicate and slightly scented, best with a slice of lemon.
Ichang	Dark brown and the most similar to Indian teas.
Bohea	A black tea from the North of China.
Lapsang Souchong	Light grey-green in colour with a distinctive aroma and pungent, smoky and tarry flavour – best with lemon rather than milk.
Yunnan	A deep toned and golden colour from western China, its delicacy makes it ideal for iced tea.

Speciality

Old Hyson and Gunpowder	Varieties of green tea, with a slightly bitter flavour.
Oolong	A cross between a black and green tea. This has a delicate, soft peach-like flavour.
Earl Grey	Unusual blend of large China and Darjeeling, delicately scented with the oil of Bergamot. Brought back from China by the 2nd Earl Grey in 1830.
Lady Londonderry	Blend of Ceylon, India and Formosa (Taiwan) teas used by a society hostess in the first half of the 20th century.
Lemon Tea	A blend of Ceylon teas mixed with lemon peel and scented with lemon essence that can be served hot or cold.
Russian Tea	A long-leafed tea grown in the foothills of the Caucasian mountains, best drunk with a slice of lemon.
Jasmine Tea	Chinese tea scented with dried jasmine petals, and should be drunk weak with a slice of lemon.
Orange Pekoe	A smooth blend of Ceylon teas where the orange refers to the colour rather than the flavour.